CRASHWORTHINESS
OF
VEHICLES

CRASHWORTHINESS
OF
VEHICLES

An Introduction to Aspects of Collision of
Motor Cars, Ships, Aircraft, and Railway Coaches

W. JOHNSON and A. G. MAMALIS

Department of Engineering
University of Cambridge
Cambridge, England

MECHANICAL ENGINEERING PUBLICATIONS LTD
LONDON

First published 1978

ISBN 0 85298 386 7

Printed in Great Britain by David Green (Printers) Ltd., Kettering
Bound by Heffers Printers Ltd., Cambridge

CONTENTS

PREFACE

The introduction which follows sufficiently describes our views and limited aims in presenting this elementary monograph on Crashworthiness. Essentially it comprises the material of a few lectures given towards the end of a course on Impact to final year undergraduates in Engineering. It is intended to illustrate and indicate the engineering design outlets and applications of the analytical work of their course – mainly on stress waves and plastic deformation – and to introduce them to the literature, and new notions and considerations in engineering impact situations. We hope that the contents of our work will be of value and help to students, teachers and many kinds of professional engineers.

Inconsistencies and imprecision may be noted at various points in the text; this is due to our wish to present information from original references in its pristine form.

Cambridge
24 September 1977

W. JOHNSON
A. G. MAMALIS

ACKNOWLEDGEMENTS

The authors are greatly indebted to the many newspapers, magazines, journals and research institutes for the various figures and photographs reproduced below; their source will be readily identified through the references given.

We should like to thank Dr S. R. Reid and Dr A. Williams for reading our manuscript and for making many useful comments and suggestions.

We are also very grateful to Miss Lorraine Willis for typing our manuscript and to Mr E. D. Nisbet and Mr J. D. Read for their help in reproducing our photographs and diagrams.

INTRODUCTION

Public concern about safety and in particular public demand for better protection against injury from vehicles undergoing collision, has become increasingly vocal in recent years. In every country the fraction of population which is educated increases yearly, so that the attention given to the traumatic events in which it is sometimes involved annually enlarges; people are also increasingly better informed technically. Perhaps starting from motor cars, the mass agitation for better passive† safety has now grown to include aircraft and, to a lesser extent, other vehicles also. Damage and loss of life in aircraft and rail disasters is nearly always on a relatively large scale and is therefore, newsworthy and attention-demanding; concern about spoiling the marine and littoral environment at large, has made ship collisions a frequent topic of important public concern.

Mitigating or reducing collision damage and redressing its consequences is now also a matter of widespread interest in its legal, commercial, and insurance aspects.

The purpose of this review is to bring together easily obtained but widely scattered knowledge or information about aspects of the mechanics of vehicular impact, of the plastic deformation processes which result, and the consequences for human passengers; how these destructive consequences can be reduced or minimized when a collision occurs is our major concern.

The literature on these latter topics is vast and is growing very rapidly – for example, there are annual conferences on automobile crash situations and design mechanics and the American Society of Automotive Engineers' Twentieth Stapp Car Crash Conference held in October 1976 resulted in 814 pages of proceedings; see ref. (1) on p. 57.

A deep comprehensive review of crashworthiness is not feasible in relatively few pages, and in any case, is rendered difficult because the subject matter has not yet been reduced to, or organized as a discipline in the accepted scientific sense. The intention of the authors is, however, to try to give a connected and reasonably co-ordinated review of the English language work which is available for examination; our monograph attempts primarily to expose facets of the subject and thus to quicken and develop interest in it. The field, besides being of growing significance to the public at large, in itself merits greater attention and interest from the mass of professional engineers and engineering teachers. ‡ Vehicle

† For definition, see p. 36.   ‡ As does the whole subject of impact mechanics.

impact processes are very complex events, where the simultaneous structural response of many different, interacting units renders individual behaviour only rarely susceptible to the usual detailed analysis associated with a single component, and to which the engineering or mechanics student is (often unfortunately) habituated. Many features of these processes, at this stage in the early history of this new subject, have to be approached in a primitive or elementary manner, often making use of ordinarily reported events; when professional engineering attention is directed to investigating them, sophisticated inquiry tends to manifest itself in testing, experimentation, and modelling – not detailed, theoretical analysis.

The book by Sir Alfred Pugsley, *The Safety of Structures*, ref. (2), p. 57, is recommended reading, especially for its wide philosophical statements and its discussion of the real engineering problems touching safety which can face a senior designer or chief engineer; it is also interesting to contrast the extensive technical progress or developments reflected in this review (and in ref. (6)), and achieved over the last decade, with that examined in Pugsley's chapter on 'Dynamic Loads on Structures'.

THE STRUCTURE OF THE REVIEW

We review vehicular impact under the headings of the four main classes of vehicle: motor cars, aircraft, ships, railway coaches – and lifts or elevators. Broadly, we consider damage to the structure, and damage or injury to the persons transported: since these two aspects are interconnected, the subject of crashworthiness brings a new dimension into structural design considerations.

Our review is intended to provide an introduction to this relatively new topic for professional engineers when they are required to encounter it for the first time; it will acquaint them with some sources of literature and introduce them to terms and concepts found in it. We appreciate that shortcomings in this review may be apparent to engineers already fully occupied with these problems but, we believe, notwithstanding that, our survey constitutes a reasonably well-balanced synopsis of the whole topic. It is also our hope to be writing for engineering students, to provide them with a first exposure to the subject and thus create an awareness of it which they will carry into later professional life.

THREE USEFUL SIMPLE NOTIONS

1. The multi-collisional situation for transported bodies

Any transporting body may usefully be thought of as consisting of a bounding envelope of fixed or well-defined outer shape, and the contents which are to be carried. To reduce damage during transit, minimum relative velocity between the envelope and its contents is required throughout the whole journey. In a collision it is the envelope which first suffers the impact and undergoes damage locally in the impact region, or remotely as with spalling (see Fig. 29). The contents only later suffer the effects of the impact; they continue to move as the envelope is arrested and, depending on their nature, distribution (and attachments) within the envelope, are later involved in secondary collisions with the inner surface of the envelope or other portions of the contents. The encounter of the envelope with an external body is the first collision, and subsequent collisions undergone by the contents within the envelope are collectively referred to as the second collision.

When a driven car undergoes collision it is the car surface envelope or exterior which is first arrested by an external object; this is the first collision. The driver (and other persons or objects) may later impinge with fixtures to the inside of the envelope (e.g., steering column and dashboard etc.), and probably injury follows; this is a second collision.†

The driver himself may, however, be considered as an 'envelope and contents' – largely in respect of his head. Damage to the skull may be regarded as damage to an envelope and, due to the semi-liquid nature of the brain and its ability to transmit stress waves or undergo sloshing inside its bony container, the brain contents may also undergo damage; this would be a third collision. The set of phenomena may be referred to as a three-collision situation. The outer surface of any moving body undergoes the primary collision and consecutively the contents within sustain the secondary and subsequent collisions.

Many complex collision processes may be seen as consecutive envelope–body contents collisions, e.g., a crate of eggs being carried by a lorry may be involved in a four-collision situation.

† Many facets of structural safety design (or lack of it) in motor cars are discussed at length by Nader in Chapter 3 of his book (3), under the heading of 'The Second Collision'.

2. Impact crushing of vehicles: retardation rate and vehicle length

A long, moving, uniform tubular structure colliding end-on with a flat, stationary body will experience a resisting force $F = \sigma A$, where σ is the mean crushing stress for the structure and A its cross-sectional area. The mass of the structure is ρAL where ρ is its density and L its length. Thus, the uniform retardation f is $\sigma A / \rho AL = \sigma / \rho L$. Hence, if structures differ only in length, the retardation arising in collisions, with this idealized approach, would be inversely proportional to their length. If passenger injury is assumed to arise from a retardation which is too great, then this last expression implies that ships are relatively safe, railway coaches and aircraft† somewhat less so, and that motor cars are dangerous.

3. Impulsive loading of a plane rigid body: the circle of constant acceleration

It is instructive and useful to recall an elementary result for the impulsive loading in its own plane of a two-dimensional rigid body as in Fig. 1; the

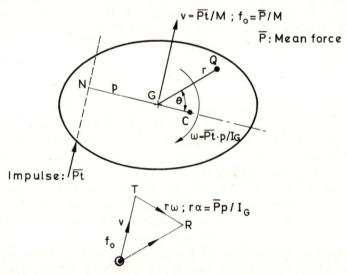

Fig. 1. Impulsive loading in its own plane of a two-dimensional rigid body

† The introduction of wide-body aeroplanes, e.g., the DC-10 and the Tristar (approximate dimensions: length 55 m (180 ft), wingspan 47 m (155 ft), and height 18 m (58 ft), weighing 315 tons when fully loaded) puts them more into the class of ships, except that when they are at their most hazardous – take off and landing – they are moving at about 240 km/h (150 miles/h).

14

situation has similarities with that of the sudden, 'point' loading of a vehicle which suffers a transverse collision or blow. The blow or impulse $\overline{Pt}$, where in

$$\overline{Pt} = \int_0^t P dt,$$

P denotes force and t, time causes a change in the velocity of translation of the body v in the direction of the blow of $\overline{Pt}/M$, where M is the mass of the body; it also gives rise to a change in angular velocity, $\omega = \overline{Pt} \cdot p/I_G$, where $p = GN$, is the perpendicular distance from the centroid on to the line of the blow and I_G is the moment of inertia of M about G.

The total linear acceleration f_T of a point Q in the body at distance r from G is the vector sum of f_0 and ra where f_0 is the mean linear acceleration of G equal to $\overline{P}/M$ and a is the mean angular acceleration equal to $\overline{P} \cdot p/I_G = f_0 p/k_g^2$; k_g denotes the radius of gyration of M about G. From Fig. 1,

$$f_{yy} = f_0(1 - pr \cos \theta/k_g^2)$$

and

$$f_{xx} = f_0 pr \sin \theta/k_g^2;$$

thus

$$f_T^2/f_0^2 = 1 + (pr/k_g^2)^2 - (2pr \cos \theta/k_g^2) = c^2.$$

Hence,

$$\left(\frac{r}{k_g} - \frac{\cos \theta}{p/k_g}\right)^2 = \frac{c^2 - 1 + \cos^2\theta}{(p/k_g)^2}$$

If we choose a constant fraction for c, then the last equation represents a circle whose centre is at C, where $GC = k_g^2/p$, and is of radius ck_g^2/p.

At a point C on NG produced ($GC = k_g^2/p$) where $c = 0$, the acceleration is zero and the whole body can thus be thought of as turning about it; C is the Centre of Percussion and a thin shaft through the body at C would experience no impulse since the body would not move and bear on the shaft at that point.

From the equation above it is clear that all points within a circle of centre C and radius $ck_g{}^2/p$ undergo an acceleration of cf_0 at most. If, then, it is desired that a body or instrument must not be subjected to an acceleration of more than cf_0 it should be placed inside this circle. An example is shown in Fig. 2 of how the location and extent of the circle varies with the position of the blow for a rectangular ring of constant weight per unit length, when $c = \frac{1}{2}$.

For a straight uniform rod, of length l, struck a blow at one end $GC = l/3$. Due to the distribution of linear acceleration along the rod, a bending moment is set up at each section, which is greatest at $l/3$ from G towards the blow (4).

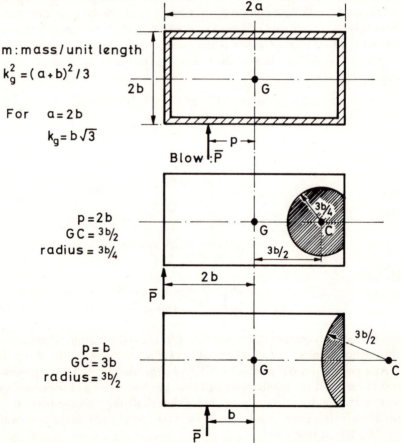

Fig. 2. Circles of constant acceleration for a uniformly thin rectangular ring, $c = \frac{1}{2}$

16

Part I: Principally on motor car collisions

It is difficult to discuss motor car collision design in full since this has drawn increasing attention during the last ten years or so. Not only is the volume of such activity now very large but the varieties of it are also different as between different manufacturers. The number of components to which considerable crashworthy design attention is *not* given is large and such matters only become evident when unwanted accidents occur.

The aspects outlined below have been assembled from easily available information and give a general view of what is currently being attempted, the standards being achieved, and the considerations involved.

Whilst some motor car manufacturers have long endeavoured to engineer safety against impact into their models (e.g., Mercedes and Volvo), attention to vehicle safety design seems first to have been highlighted, and great attention drawn to it, by Ralph Nader in 1964 in his book *Unsafe at Any Speed* (3); the updated 1973 edition is well worth perusal.

Main types of impact

The main types of impact involving cars and lorries have been tabulated by Franchini (5) (Fig. 3). A full analysis of several of these cases, using elementary rigid body mechanics, has been given by Grime and Jones (6); their comprehensive paper, besides containing much detailed information about crashes, also examines the manner in which a vehicle comes to injure an occupant.

Head-on collisions with barriers or between cars moving with the same speed, in the range 40–72 km/h (25–45 miles/h), for many British cars show a time for retardation of about 0·1 s with an approximately linear rise to, and fall from, a greatest retardation of about 40 g, which occurs after about 0·05 s, and involves a crushing distance of about 0·6 m (2 ft) for each car. The mean crushing strength of a car is probably 206 kN/m² (30 lbf/in²) of its minimum cross-sectional area, say 1·5 m² (16 ft²).† From results in ref. (6) it may be deduced that the crushing distance for British cars in frontal collision with a rigid barrier is approxi-

---

† If the crushing distance $s = 0·6$ m (2 ft) and the initial speed $u = 30$ miles/h (13·4 m/s), then using $u^2 = 2fs$, where f denotes the uniform retardation, $13·4^2 = 2 \times 0·6 \times f$, and $f = 150$ m/s² $\simeq 15$ g. Also with $v = u + ft$, $13·4 = 150$ t and hence $t = 0·088$, say 1/10th s.

mately given by, s (in inches) $= 1\cdot2v - 10$, where v is the speed at impact in miles/h.

For a car 5·26 m (14 ft) long, 1·53 m (5 ft) wide and weight 10·5 kN (2350 lbf), it is easily shown using the equations of momentum, that for

LOAD	IMPACT		OBSTACLE	TYPE
BACKWARD	DISTRIBUTED	head on		1
		front end, offset		2
	CONCENTRATED	wedging of passenger car under truck.		3
		truck cab front end panel head on.		4
FORWARD	DISTRIBUTED	rear end, full on		5
		forward displacement of bulky goods or loose gravel, etc.		6
	CONCENTRATED	rear end, offset		7
		forward displacement of logs, poles, etc.		8

(a) Main types of impact; longitudinal load

18

LOAD	IMPACT	OBSTACLE	TYPE
DISTRIBUTED	side, 90°	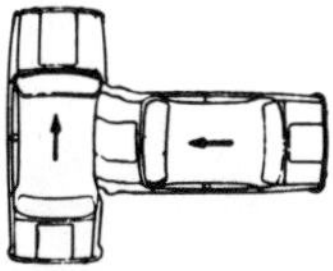	9
CONCENTRATED	side, oblique		10
	side skid against tree, pole, etc.	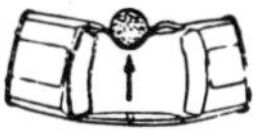	11

(b) Main types of impact; transverse load

LOAD	IMPACT	OBSTACLE	TYPE
DISTRIBUTED	full area, roof panel.		12
CONCENTRATED	side edge, roof panel.		13
	end edge, roof panel.	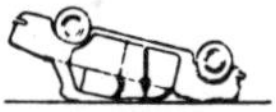	14

(c) Main types of impact; vertical load

Fig. 3. Main types of impact, (a) *longitudinal load,* (b) *transverse load,* (c) *vertical load*

rigid body impact with an immovable barrier at P, e.g., a tree (Fig. 4), that,

$$-\overline{Xt} = M(u - u_0) \tag{1}$$

$$-\overline{Yt} = Mv \tag{2}$$

$$\text{and} \quad \overline{Xt} \cdot d - \overline{Yt} \cdot a/2 = I_G \cdot \omega. \tag{3}$$

19

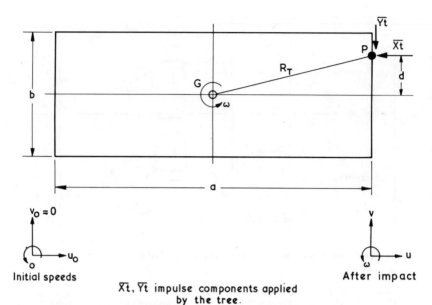

Initial speeds

$\overline{Xt}, \overline{Yt}$ impulse components applied by the tree.

After impact

Fig. 4. Rigid body impact with an immovable barrier at P, e.g., a tree

Assuming the car rotates about P, with angular speed ω, then $u = \omega \cdot d$ and $v = -a\omega/2$ and after substituting in (3) and simplifying,

$$\omega = u_0 \cdot \frac{d}{I_G/M + R_T^2} ; \qquad (4)$$

I_G is the moment of inertia of the car about its centre of gravity G and R_T the distance of P from G. Assuming $I_G = M(a^2 + b^2)/12$,

$$\omega = u_0 \frac{12d}{a^2 + b^2 + 12R_T^2} . \qquad (5)$$

If impact takes place at 30 miles/h (44 ft/s), $\omega = 1{\cdot}23$ rad/s. Also, if the tree penetrates 0·6 m (2 ft) into the car and its retardation is uniform, then, as above, the retardation is $\simeq 15$ g and the time of impact is $\simeq 0{\cdot}09$ s. Supposing the car to rotate about P and to be brought to rest at a uniform rate, the angular retardation rate and its amount of rotation are respectively $1{\cdot}23/0{\cdot}09 \simeq 13{\cdot}5$ rad/s² and $1{\cdot}23^2/2 \times 13{\cdot}5 \simeq 3°$. The rotational kinetic energy immediately after impact as a fraction of the initial kinetic energy of the car is $12(a^2 + b^2)d^2/(a^2 + b^2 + 12R_T{}^2)^2$ – which in this instance is nearly zero.

CAR COLLISION TESTS

1. Test tracks

Highly instrumented full-size cars (carrying strain gauges and transducers etc.) are now frequently tested by towing them on test tracks, or by using radio guidance, into nominally rigid barriers (often concrete) to observe (photographically) and measure the plastic deformation (local and diffused) caused, and the load–time pulses brought to bear on various parts of the body structure. Crash test facilities to study angled impact (Fig. 5), and impact with bridge parapets, motorway barriers, and lamp

Fig. 5. An angled impact

standards are common. Figure 6 shows a typical record of reduction in retardation rate, with distance behind a front bumper, in a 56 km/h (35 miles/h) head-on impact into a barrier (7).

2. Test sleds and catapults

Test sleds, with a 4·45 kN (1000 lbf) load, propelled by linear induction motors at up to 64 km/h (40 miles/h) have been developed and are frequently used for studying secondary impacts, e.g., as between a modelled passenger (a dummy) and a steering column and instrument panel. Seat performance is also fairly easily assessed in this circumstance (Figs 7 and 8).

3. Free-fall

Originally, free-fall tests on motor cars were adopted in order to simulate

21

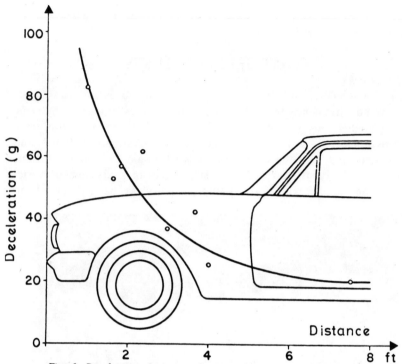

Fig. 6. *Deceleration decay as a function of distance from front bumper*

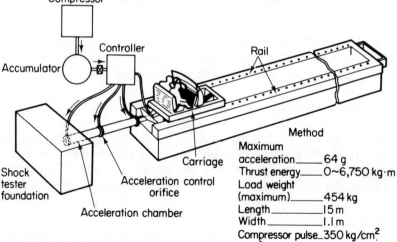

Fig. 7. *A schematic diagram showing the experimental set-up of test sleds*

Method

Maximum acceleration	64 g
Thrust energy	0~6,750 kg·m
Load weight (maximum)	454 kg
Length	15 m
Width	1.1 m
Compressor pulse	350 kg/cm²

Fig. 8. A test sled

head-on collisions but have now been abandoned; they have been resumed to study the effect of vertical loads on roofs in roll-over situations.

4. *Pendulum*
Tests using the easily measured, concentrated blow delivered by the weight of a swinging pendulum, seem to have been first introduced in Sweden for tests on tractor frames (see p. 31); it has also been proposed for use in evaluating car-bumper designs.

5. *Static tests*
This refers to the slow static compression of a car between instrumented rams.

SOME STRUCTURAL FEATURES RELEVANT TO COLLISIONS

A general review
This topic, in general terms, i.e., structural response to impact, has important and widespread application; the reader is referred to an excellent review which contains a section specifically devoted to motor cars, by Rawlings (8).

Plastic failure of tubes and struts in compression

The literature on the buckling of solid struts and thin-walled tubes, of circular or non-circular section, when subjected to static or dynamic axial compression, is extremely large and relevant structural analysis is called for in many fields of engineering, besides that of vehicle impact. See for example, refs (9–15) and see also p. 109.

Postlethwaite and Mills (16) and others have investigated theoretically the retardation with time of a mass impinging on the end of a *strut* (at about 10 m/s), and this happens typically as in Fig. 9. There are pre- and post-failure buckling regions; the strut is supposed compressed axially until the load is sufficient to overcome any plastic bending moment generated and the effects of lateral inertia of the material.

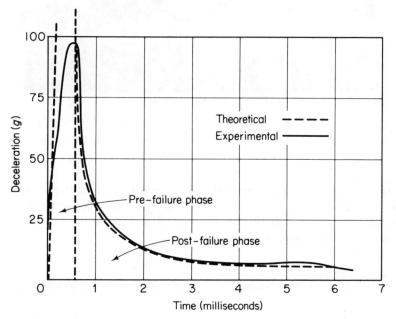

Fig. 9. The deceleration signature of a mass in axial impact on the end of a strut

In ref. (16), besides investigating integral tubes the authors reported on examinations of the compression of tubes containing cut-outs (Fig. 10). They reached the very interesting conclusion that statically loaded tubes containing cut-outs (for all but the smallest apertures) failed in the region

24

Fig. 10. Discontinuous tube statically loaded

of discontinuity but, under dynamic testing, except where the cut-out portion exceeded 50 per cent of the tube circumference, plastic failure always occurred at the impacted end, as for an uncut tube; this difference in behaviour was attributed to the effect of longitudinal inertia (10). Interpreting this work with respect to wheel-arches, which are seldom more than one half of the wing perimeter, and particularly as they are lipped and strengthened, it is suggested that, in general, this discontinuity can be neglected when considering dynamic loading.

The impact response of curved box-columns, Fig. 11, involving large overall and local deformation, has been studied by Ni (17), who observed significant changes in energy absorbing performance with speed of impact; this, and Macaulay and Redwood (11), and Redwood's own

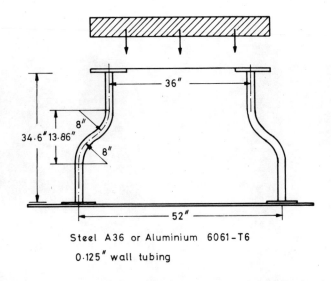

Steel A36 or Aluminium 6061-T6

0.125″ wall tubing

Fig. 11. (a) *Dimensions of the structures under consideration*

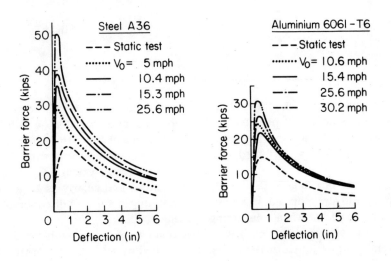

Fig. 11.(b) *The effects of impact speed on dynamic force–deflection relationship*

26

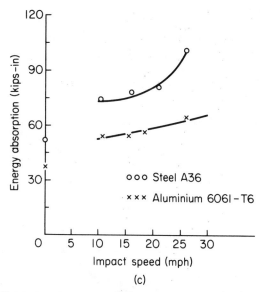

Fig. 11. (c) *The effects of impact speed on energy absorption*

observations **(12)**, are somewhat in contrast with the work described in ref. **(16)**.

Miles **(18)** has given a useful analysis for predicting force–large deflection curves for thin-walled beam structures in plastic bending; see his typical Fig. 12 and also refs **(19–21)**.

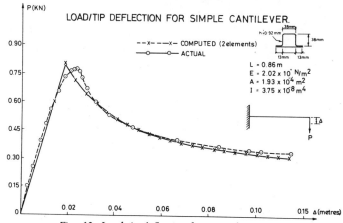

Fig. 12. Load-tip-deflection for a simple cantilever

Non-metallic car bodies

Early on, fibre-reinforced plastic car bodies, when involved in collisions, were found to disintegrate and to be especially vulnerable to side impacts. Their design and performance has been greatly improved to be comparable to, and sometimes better than, steel body cars.

Energy absorbing frames

Figure 13 shows a diagram of an energy absorbing S-frame which consists of heavy box members, as made known in 1969. Inset in the figure is the crash-front S-frame before and after a frontal impact. An elastic stress distribution for a large curvature beam was assumed for the design of this frame, using a static ultimate strength for the material of 345 MN/m² (50 000 lbf/in²); see also ref. (22).

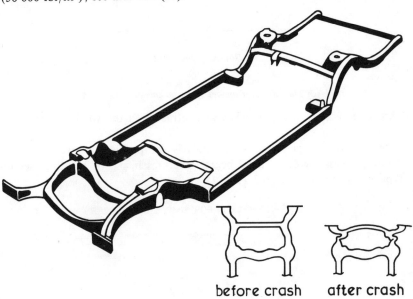

before crash   after crash

Fig. 13. Energy absorbing frame

Crumple zones†

In ref. (24), p. 25 the following experimental facts are noted:

(a) that front and rear ends, in the case of frontal or rear end collision respectively, 'collapse and absorb energy before the centre portion deforms permanently',

† See the recent paper by Saczalski and Angus, pp. 1–16, in ref. (21) of Part III.

28

(b) 'approximately 90 per cent of the energy goes into permanent and 10 per cent into elastic deformation'.

Many manufacturers of cars now design into their models regions at the front (but behind the bumper) and rear of the car, which crumple on collision in a controlled fashion at a preselected rate thereby reducing the forces or the retardation rate which a passenger may have to bear (Fig. 14).

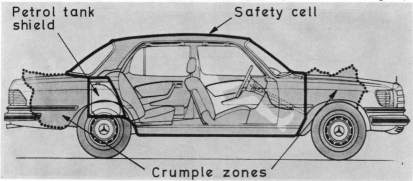

Fig. 14. Rigid passenger cell with impact absorbing crumple zones

Bumpers

Bumper designs are manifold.[†] In 1973 all cars sold in the USA were required to be able to withstand an 8 km/h (5 miles/h) frontal impact without damage to the lights; typically in some models curved over-riders encased in rubber have been fitted.

Bumper mountings which have been tried include strong ribbed steel cones which concertina under impact (like camera bellows), and hydraulic mountings (water is ejected through fine holes as the rams are forced back by the impulse); see Fig. 15(a).

Bumpers in the 'best' cars are often now covered with resilient plastic layers in order, among other things, to mitigate injuries to pedestrians and cyclists. It has recently been reported that[‡] 'the bumpers, front and rear, are of steel, covered with flexible honeycomb plastic which does not lie directly on the steel backing but is supported by ribs. The energy absorbing qualities have been improved so that soon after impact the plastic reforms to its original shape. If the impact is of greater severity,

[†] See the article (23) on the 'beer can' bumper design, which consisted of twenty-three beer and soda cans (weight 0·34 kg) between parallel boards, entered in the Urban Vehicle Design Competition by students of Arizona University; the criterion was the arrest with no damage of a head-on impact by a car moving at 5 miles/h.
[‡] *Guardian*, 14 Nov. 1977.

the plastic cladding can be cheaply replaced.' An interesting example of the ability of certain kinds of plastics materials in tubular form to recover their shape completely after a large amount of compression and then immersion in hot water has been shown in ref. (9), see also Fig. 15(b).

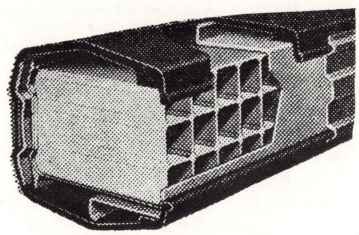

Fig. 15. (a) *Bumpers that can take an impact up to 8 km/h (5 miles/h) up front (up to 4 km/h in the rear) and return to their original shape*

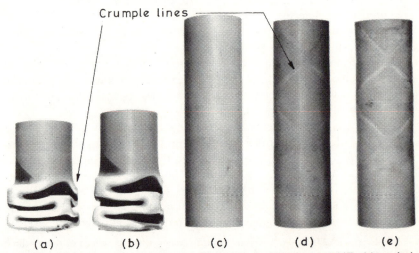

Crumple lines

(a)   (b)   (c)   (d)   (e)

Fig. 15. (b) *Crushed and recovered PVC tubes (thickness/diameter = 0·067); (a) crushed by impact; (b) crushed quasi-statically; (c) undeformed specimen; (d) impact specimen (a) after recovery; (e) quasi-static specimen (b) after recovery*

30

Car roof

To protect passengers against crushing it has been proposed in the USA that car roofs must not collapse when they fall from a height of 0·6 m (2 ft) by more than 100 mm (4 in); this standard is met by some designs.

Driver and passenger compartment or safety cell

The 'survival space' or a minimum residual space after impact, which envelops occupants taking account of occupant size, driving posture, and seats appears to be almost constant regardless of car model. It has been suggested that in this space all profiles be rounded to a radius of more than 100 mm – to accommodate the rounded profile of the head etc. Franchini (5) states that designed maintenance of survival space for collision speeds of at least up to 48 km/h (30 miles/h) is generally possible.

Strong steel compartments – cages or safety cells – are frequently now designed into cars, see Fig. 14; the passengers are protected from above and below, between the front and rear bumpers and from the sides. The sound functioning of the cell depends on good bumper and crumple zone design. See also ref. (25).

Safety frames for tractors

Early work in Scandinavia was devoted to the design of a framework, to be fitted to tractors, to give a driver protection when roll-over occurred. Test set-ups involve a pendulum weight impact device as in Fig. 16. Safety-frame legislation (1970) and testing procedures (1968) are laid down by the British Standards Institution; see also refs (26) and (27).

Car collisions with breakaway obstacles

Attempts to design effective structures, such as road signs and lamp-posts, which will break away when struck by cars have been made by California and Pennsylvania Highways Departments and at Cornell and Texas Universities.† Since the conditions of impact which can arise are multi-parameter, any full scale experimental testing is thus very expensive. By establishing scale model conditions and with a new approach to applying the methods of dimensional analysis, it was shown to be possible to employ scale models to design-in improvements which were verified by full-scale

† Whilst breakaway structures may reduce injury to the car driver they can nevertheless constitute a very serious hazard to pedestrians in the vicinity. Thus their desirability depends upon an assessment of local circumstances; they should not be introduced until everything has been done to protect the car passengers such as providing seat belts and crumple zones etc.

31

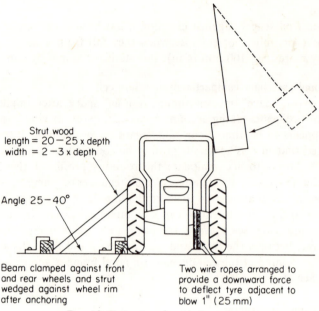

Strut wood
length = 20 − 25 x depth
width = 2 − 3 x depth

Angle 25 − 40°

Beam clamped against front
and rear wheels and strut
wedged against wheel rim
after anchoring

Two wire ropes arranged to
provide a downward force
to deflect tyre adjacent to
blow 1" (25 mm)

Fig. 16. Test set-up for side impact

counterparts. Interesting sequences for collisions with signposts and lamp-posts are shown in Fig. 17; see also ref. (**28**).

Modelling

In the last section we referred to the use of models for car–obstacle impact studies but scale modelling is explored in greater depth by Holmes and Sliter (**29**). They show that scale models can be used to study the response of complex structures – displacements, acceleration, buckling and fracture, etc. – for cars, buses, trucks, and railway vehicles. Cost-effectiveness particularly is assessed *vis-à-vis* full scale tests. It is claimed that small-scale tests (optimum scale 1/4 to 1/10) can be built and tested at 1/3 to 1/4 of the cost of equivalent full scale tests, and the time required is less than one third; Fig. 18 shows on a bar chart some of the overall economics of scale-testing.

Holmes and Colton (**30**) after model-testing, assert that simple box section bumpers of 60 lbf (267 N), or less at 50 lbf (222 N) with aluminium, interacting with an energy absorbing frame and impinging against a rigid pole at 50 miles/h (80 km/h) (a constant retardation of 40 *g* over about 2 ft (0·6 m)) can bring car occupants to rest without serious injury.

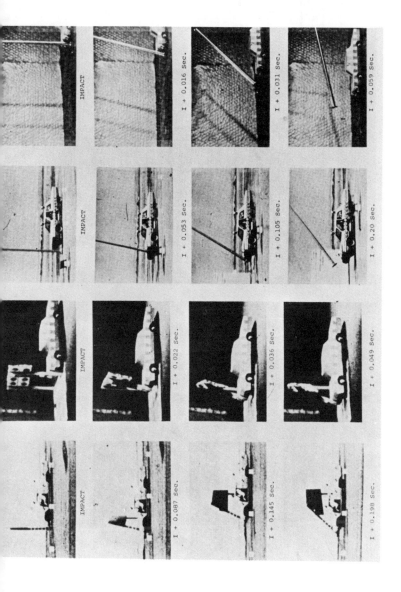

Fig. 17. (a) Collision of 1964 Dodge with a signpost at 61 km/h (38 miles/h) and model collision at 14·4 km/h (9 miles/h)
(b) Collision of 1966 Dodge with a lightpost at 65 km/h (40·4 miles/h) and model collision at 12·9 km/h (8 miles/h)

33

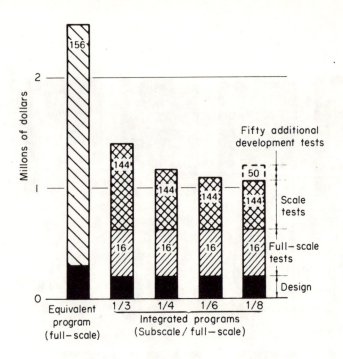

Fig. 18. Cost of programmes at various scale factors

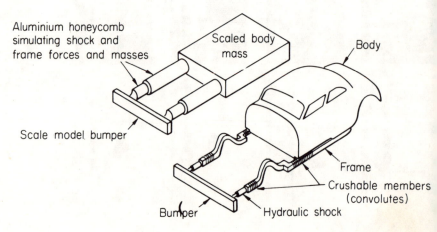

Fig. 19. One company's conception of a safety vehicle and a dynamic model

34

The model and an envisaged full scale prototype design are shown in Fig. 19.

Professor M. C. Shaw (in his unpublished notes: 'Introduction to Engineering', Carnegie–Mellon University), has discussed modelling the performance of a crash barrier (scale 1 to 25) which consists of an array of twenty-six 55-gallon steel drums; in a head-on collision, the car would be arrested over a considerable distance. The modelled drums were of aluminium, 25·4 mm (1 in) diameter, 356 mm (14 in) long and 0·076 mm (0·003 in) thick, whilst the prototype drum was about 0·61 m (2 ft) diameter, 0·91 m (3 ft) high and 267 N (60 lbf) weight (Fig. 20).

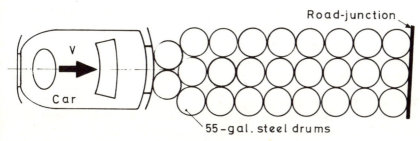

Fig. 20. (a) *Crash barrier of steel drums*

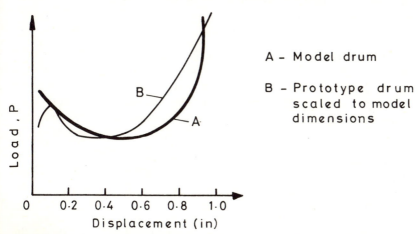

A – Model drum

B – Prototype drum scaled to model dimensions

Fig. 20. (b) *Comparison of load-displacement curves for model and prototype drums*

PASSENGER ARRESTING COMPONENTS: PASSIVE SAFETY FEATURES

For the past ten years the UK has had a stable number of fatalities per year at 7–8000. Accident patterns in every country are not always the same. In the UK, pedestrians and car occupants each constitute 40 per cent of its fatalities† but in the USA, pedestrians are only 17 per cent of the population of fatalities (26). In the UK a large proportion of fatal accidents involve cars with commercial vehicles.

Active safety and passive safety
Accident avoidance, or active safety, includes improvement of vision limitations, braking, tyres, handling, and aspects of driver control; the economic benefit of such measures is unknown. Passive safety refers to reducing the frequency and severity of a particular injury to a road user when once the event has occurred – not necessarily fatalities, e.g. windscreens and facial damage. Passive safety features involve the following:

1. *Seat belts*
Since 1961, investigations of the use of diagonal and lap belts have been shown to be beneficial in 30–55 per cent of cases; this applies much more for frontal than side impacts. The effectiveness of three-point belts is well established. The interaction of seat belt anchorages and internal structures, e.g., the lack of adequate centre posts for sound attachment, is discussed by Nader (3) (p. 109).

2. *Anti-burst door latches*
Ejection through a door space in a collision is a major source of fatal and serious injury. On British motorways 56 per cent of fatalities (1964) were by ejection, but the environment in which they occur also matters (only 4 per cent in urban collisions). The introduction cf these door latches was a significant, but still a largely unrecognized, improvement in vehicle collision protection.

3. *Energy absorbing (E.A.) steering column assemblies*
Stimulating background reading to energy absorbing (E.A.) steering column assembly performance is to be had from Nader's book, ref. (3) pp. 76–85, from which Fig. 21 is taken.

† For the same number of miles driven, as between cars and lorries, the heavier the vehicle the more the number of fatalities in which it is likely to be involved.

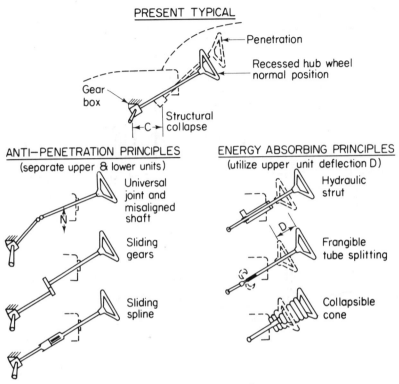

PRESENT TYPICAL

Penetration

Recessed hub wheel
normal position

Gear box

Structural collapse

C

ANTI–PENETRATION PRINCIPLES
(separate upper & lower units)

Universal joint and misaligned shaft

N

Sliding gears

Sliding spline

ENERGY ABSORBING PRINCIPLES
(utilize upper unit deflection D)

Hydraulic strut

D

Frangible tube splitting

Collapsible cone

Fig. 21. Steering assembly

These columns are required to fulfil two purposes:

(a) when there is rearward intrusion of the column into the driving space it is supposed to be restricted and,

(b) a limited load only is allowed to be applied to the driver, and, when reached, there is progressive collapse so that he has a tolerable 'ride-down'.

Measurable benefits from such steering columns are not in fact seen; it is maintained that non-axial loading is usual and this tends to nullify the value of these devices.

Early considered designs of inversion tube for maintaining a constant ride-down force are shown in Fig. 22.

Initially, work on E.A. steering assembly design for safety was related to the unrestrained driver and early promising results have not been

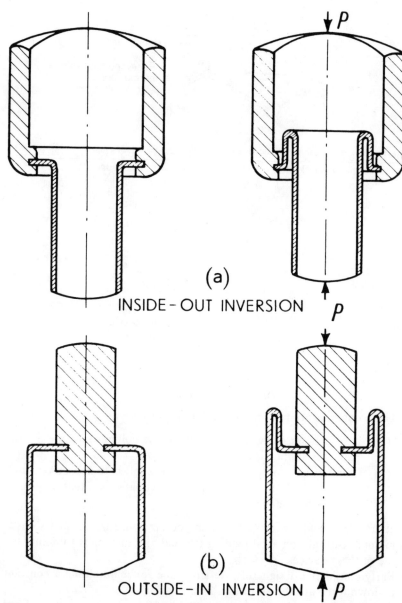

(a)
INSIDE - OUT INVERSION

(b)
OUTSIDE - IN INVERSION

Fig. 22. Sectioned invertubes showing tube and arrangements: (a) External, inside-out inversion; (b) Internal, outside-in inversion

fulfilled. For the USA it is claimed that the use of the E.A. column may in fact be associated with a rise in the number of head injuries and the E.A. column advantage is marked only for high-speed impacts. Typical column collapse loads are 6 to 11 kN with rearward penetration of 127 mm. For some UK cars it seems that high angle columns are associated with a low incidence of serious chest injury for front wheel drive cars. The column is also very directional in its properties and only collapses as intended if struck within a fairly small angular range.

Steering columns that collapse in several selected regions, together with a universal joint that keeps a driver in control, are now on the market.

4. *Head restraints and seats*

Non-adjustable head restraints are said to be worth installing principally for protection against rear collision and so that the frequency of cervical spine injuries is reduced. Females are said to be more susceptible to 'whip-lash' injuries than males.

Since 55 per cent of car impacts are frontal and 8 per cent are to the rear, some account should be taken of the possibility of a rear seat occupant striking his head on the rear of any head restraint.

Seat mounting failures are frequent and the present average 20 g standard does not prevent them. Special attention, now devoted to some designs of anchorage, ensures that seat loads of up to 3 tons can be tolerated.

5. *Windscreen glass*

This was the first passive safety feature to be introduced forty years ago.

Toughened glass windscreens are common and of long standing. The manner of toughening is illustrated in Fig. 23; ordinary glass is heated to its softening point and then rapidly air-quenched so that the two outer surfaces are forced into compression with the equilibrating stresses inside becoming tensile. Toughened glass can be made about four times as strong as ordinary glass and can withstand severe blows and temperature changes. It may easily be broken by the impact of a small stone (impact stress level determined principally by the speed of impact of the stone, not its mass), and when it occurs the release of the residual stresses causes it to craze into a mosaic of small blunt crystals which render vision impossible.

Sophisticated forms of toughened glass (Triplex Zebrazone) reduce the severity of damage and leave some residual vision.

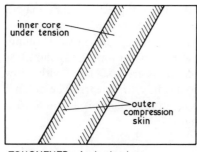
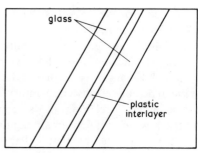

TOUGHENED : A single piece   LAMINATED : This section

(a)   (b)

Fig. 23. Windscreen; (a) *toughened,* (b) *laminated*

Laminated glass is a sandwich of two sheets of glass with a plastic membrane bonded in between, see Fig. 23. When struck by a small particle, one outer layer may crack but the damage is only local and visibility is retained; the plastic interlayer holds back the glass splinters formed. Presently, a 0·76 mm interlayer is being used and is said to be much superior to the older 0·38 mm thick layer; toughened glass is much cheaper than laminated glass but any injury level to the head and face of front seat occupants with the laminated form is claimed to be very greatly reduced. It is said that some 80 per cent of the head impacts with windscreens which occur do so at less than 58 km/h (36 miles/h); it is sometimes argued that good seat belt usage would eliminate damage or injury from windscreens. Glass not ejected but retained at the lower edge of a windscreen frame is a major source of laceration.

Laminated glass seems to have had a bad reputation in the early 1960s because an unrestrained head would punch a hole in a restrained windscreen.

Recently, a tough, transparent, polyester film (of tensile strength 8·4 kN/m (48 lbf/per in of width), in sheets 0·05 mm (0·002 in) thick and which stretches by nearly 100 per cent) has been marketed; when fixed to glass panes with adhesive they become shatter proof. Damage remains local when hit by a stone, and under blast (up to at least 76 kN/m² (11 lbf/in²) for 1 ms) the glass fragments are said to be held together by the film.

Nader (3) summarizes the requirements of a windshield as (*a*) not being so hard that the impinging head snaps back to cause fracture or concussion and (*b*) not allowing fracture and then laceration.

6. Instrument panels
These are a major source of injury due to lethal projections, sharp corners, and lack of padding; see also the remarks on p. 31 on survival space.

7. Vehicle structure
The front, rear, and side structures of cars have been developed to provide some impact attenuation and to maintain passenger compartment integrity.

8. Airbags†
The chief advantage of protective airbags is that the co-operation of the passenger is not required, i.e., they are a passive restraint system. Their disadvantages include an initial cost which is high, a firing system which may be too loud in application and unreliable in operation, be costly when requiring specialized testing and repair, and not very protective in roll-over or side-impact situations. They may also cause passenger ejection when impact is oblique; in a small car their rapid inflation could cause the internal pressure in the car to rise to a level which inflicts damage on the passengers' eardrums (175 dB at deployment has been mentioned)‡ and blows out the windows. Assessments of the cost of installed airbags in the USA were reported to be about $150 – about five times as expensive as seat belts.

Airbags systems utilize a highly compressed gas, or a pyrotechnic gas source for inflation, so that if passengers cannot quickly leave a vehicle they may be exposed to toxic emissions; guidance for design engineers, as to the degree of hazard due to this kind of toxicity, is not available.

Much discussion has taken place about the introduction of gas inflated plastic bags; a bag is inflated between the passenger and windscreen when a collision is taking place, probably having been installed in the steering hub and the car fascia; see Fig. 24. The rapid inflation is secured in a few milliseconds from a high pressure container, after frontal impact has been felt by a crash sensing device. The following sequence is suggested (31):

† Airbags are also used as rescue mats for arresting the fall of occupants jumping from burning buildings, and as pneumatic jacks for facilitating the movement of large heavy masses, e.g., immobilized aircraft.
‡ In ref. (31), levels of 150 dB are stated to have caused no permanent damage to infant squirrel monkeys when tested. Airbag noise is thought *not* to be a problem by Hickling of General Motors.

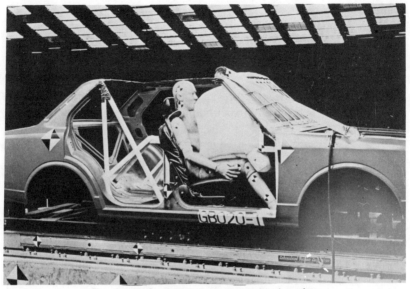

Fig. 24. Airbags performing in simulated crashes

Crash sensors depend upon the measurement of parameters such as crush, acceleration, or velocity change. Post-impact sensors utilize from 5 msec to about 2 msec of
crash data for a 48 km/h (30 mph) equivalent fixed barrier impact. In a typical
automotive barrier crash at 48 km/h (30 mph) where bumper contact occurs at
0 msec, the sensor would trigger the system at 30 msec, the air bag would deploy
at 57 msec, the forward motion of the occupant would be arrested at 95 msec, and
the forward motion of the vehicle stopped at 115 msec.

Calculations have been made to examine, by simulation, the movement
of dummy car occupants when equipped with an airbag (volume about
80 litres) in a 40 km/h collision, the airbag being located about 0·4 m
(16 in) above the hip joint. The torso, pelvis, and head first contact the
bag in that order, 50 ms after impact; the head and upper torso forward
movement is arrested after 100 ms. If a bag is located too high, the pelvis
tends to dive under the bag, i.e., 'submarining' occurs.

PEDESTRIAN PROTECTION

In nearly all pedestrian accidents, a blow is delivered by the front of a car
and fatality is caused by the primary contact rather than the secondary,
i.e., with the road surface. Vehicle shape and model influences the injury

severity; Volkswagen, it is stated, causes fewer fatalities than Cadillacs. (For the USA it is estimated that pedestrian fatalities would be reduced to $\frac{1}{4}$ or $\frac{1}{3}$ if all cars had Volkswagen characteristics!)

SEATING PROTECTION FOR PASSENGERS IN BUS COACHES

It is pointed out that in the USA the fatality rate per 100 000 000 passenger miles (1970–2) was 0·09 for buses, 0·10 for airlines, 0·28 for railways, and 2·0 for motor cars. The excellence of these figures for buses and trains is not, however, due to the provision of passenger restraint systems, or to designed-in crashworthiness.

It is useful to distinguish between the three functions which buses serve.

(a) *Intercity buses:* These have few stops, and operate at high speed often on motorways, e.g., up to 110–130 km/h (70–80 miles/h); they are designed for adults, comfort, space, and relaxation. Protection is mainly required against high-speed impact and roll-over.

(b) *Intracity buses:* These are intended for short journeys with frequent stops in city traffic, at relatively low speeds, up to say 65 km/h (40 miles/h). Easy access and short term comfort in seats are required, and standing may be allowed.

(c) *Schoolbuses:* These are not designed as such, but their functional identification with intracity buses underlines the merit of their separate consideration. Utilitarian seating and the need to accommodate simultaneously a mass of persons of very different sizes, frequently in unusual positions(!), needs to be reflected upon.

The safety features advocated for incorporation with collisions in mind are,

(i) the improvement of overturn crashworthiness and seat belts for intercity buses. (Seatbelts would prevent ejection and impact with hard interior surfaces, but are disadvantageous in roll-over situations where passengers could be anchored and suspended in circumstances difficult to escape from.)

(ii) Improvements to seat anchorages, design against window ejection and high-backed padded seats have been suggested specifically.

(iii) It is proposed that for some uses, seats be redesigned to compartmentalize the occupant in a protective cocoon. This requires energy absorbing surfaces but is limited in value to frontal crashing.

The result of a head-on collision of a bus with a concrete overpass support column at 108 km/h (67 miles/h), is shown in Fig. 25, the column penetrating 6·4 m (21 ft) into the bus. Of 45 passengers, 13 were fatally injured. The uniform retardation rate was approximately $(67 \times 22/15)^2/2 \times 21 \simeq 230$ ft/s$^2 \simeq 7$ g. The injury levels – small towards the back of the bus – should be studied in Fig. 25.

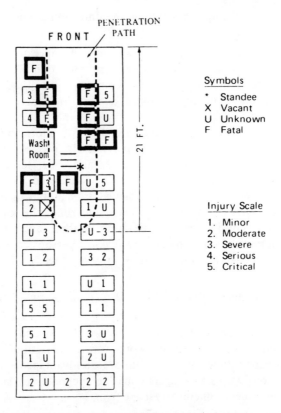

Symbols

* Standee
X Vacant
U Unknown
F Fatal

Injury Scale

1. Minor
2. Moderate
3. Severe
4. Serious
5. Critical

Fig. 25. Diagram of injuries by seating arrangement. (From Highway Accident Report NTSB-HAR-74-5, National Transportation Safety Board)

44

Seat mounting design for touring coaches has been discussed after observing the behaviour of a dummy passenger during vehicle retardation: the thighs slide forward until the knees touch the back of the seat in front, then the dummy straightens itself and moves to a standing position, the torso moving forward to contact the top of the back of the seat in front, at about chest height. A controlled movement of a seat back by crush deformation of an aluminium tube in the seat base has been designed, and also in the seat itself, by incorporating a diaphragm in the seat back where the knees impinge, so that it bends in a controlled manner.

Loads experienced by vehicles in roll-over situations are little known but a load of twice its own weight is often assumed. In agricultural tractor design, twice the tractor weight is called for, with a certain protection volume not being invaded; apparently this is fairly successful. In most accident situations, a coach is likely to roll on to the top corner before there is complete roll-over, so that corner loading could be the most severe design situation (Figs 26(a) and (b)).

Fig. 26. (a) Greyhound *bus following overturn.* (*From Highway Accident Report NTSB-HAR-73-1, National Transportation Safety Board*)

Fig. 26. (b) *The driver was killed when this single-decker bus plunged 4·5 m (15 ft) on to a beach after crashing through a seawall. None of the 33 passengers were seriously hurt.* (*Photo, Mike Evans:* The Guardian *3 February 1977.*)

Model motor coaches have been tested (32), and Fig. 27(a) shows one such before testing. Figure 27(b) shows a distributed crumpling when such a coach is axially loaded by a steadily increasing static load. Figure 27(c) shows a coach after being impact loaded on the left hand end, the more concentrated deformation at that end being clearly evident.

For comparison, Fig. 27(d) shows two thin rectangular steel tubes after axial dynamic compression as given by Postlethwaite and Mills (16); certain long and short waves were identified by them.

MOTOR CYCLES

Westcott (33) has studied the behaviour and performance of a motor cycle and the passenger mechanics in various collision situations using scaled models; he then tried to design a safety motor cycle with safety frame and protecting pillars.

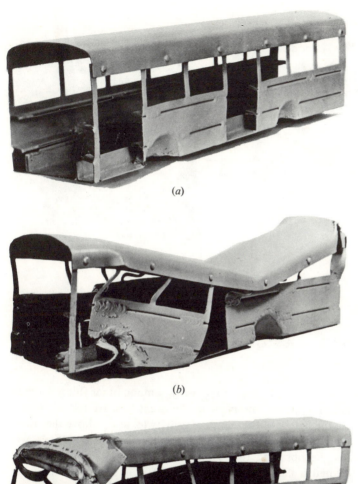

(a)

(b)

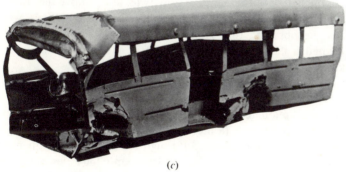

(c)

Fig. 27. A simplified model coach with windows, doors, and wheel arches: (a) original
specimen, (b) static crumpling, (c) dynamic crumpling

47

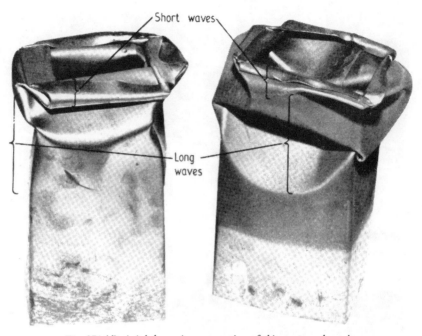

Fig. 27. (d) *Axial dynamic compression of thin rectangular tubes*

However, Ashurst in discussing this work, among other things, pointed out that since the pitching moment in the event of a frontal collision is dependent on the height of the centre of gravity (c. of g.) above the impact point – usually the wheel spindle height – larger diameter wheels were advantageous; he observed that Honda had done this with their Gold Wing, which had a flat-4 engine of low c. of g. and a fuel tank whose c. of g. is lower than normal.

A motorized tricycle
A set of tests was conducted by MIRA† (34) in which an unusual type of vehicle, an Invacar Tricycle (a motorized vehicle with bicycle steering) used by disabled drivers and obtained through the British Department of Health and Social Security, was subjected to a 48 km/h (30 miles/h) frontal barrier impact. The collapse distance of the vehicle front was 0·48 m

† Motor Industries Research Association.

(19 in); there was excessive steering system penetration and some fuel tank damage. The investigation was prompted by concern in meeting ECE regulations.

INJURY TO THE HUMAN BODY

Head injury (35)

Head injury may be sustained during collisions or emergency deceleration situations in all vehicles and is an extremely important consideration for anyone concerned in crashworthiness studies. It is desirable, therefore, to identify several of its more important aspects.

The skull–brain system is roughly that of a hard, more-or-less elastic shell containing a fairly uniformly dense substance of low modulus of rigidity; see Fig. 28.

The skull is 10 to 13 mm ($\frac{3}{8}$ to $\frac{1}{2}$ in) thick and the Caucasian brain weighs about 1500 g and is approximately 165 mm long and 140 mm wide.

The types of head component damage are,

(1) *Scalp damage:* (a) bruising,
　　　　　　　　　(b) abrasion,
　　　　　　　　　(c) lacerating.
(2) *Skull fracture:* (a) depression due to high or low speed projectile penetration,
　　　　　　　　　(b) linear or stellar,
　　　　　　　　　(c) crushing.
(3) *Extra-cerebral bleeding:* (a) a clot in the epidural space,
　　　　　　　　　　　　　　(b) a sub-dural clot in the arachnoid space.
(4) *Brain damage:* (a) concussion (alteration of consciousness or vision, etc.),
　　　　　　　　　(b) contusion (bruising): coup and contre-coup,
　　　　　　　　　(c) intercerebral haematomia (bleeding),
　　　　　　　　　(d) laceration.

Brain damage mechanisms

Note that brain damage may not be macroscopically observable, and indeed, only detectable by a clinician looking for physiological or neurological malfunction. For producing traumatic neurological deficit some suggested reasons are,

1. (a) Large compressive pressure gradients may be produced at the site of a blow as a result of linear acceleration (Fig. 28). Due to the inertia of the brain material, it 'piles-up' at the site of the blow and causes injury; but because the skull is relatively rigid, the brain material and skull tend to separate at the opposite end of the diameter causing a 'rarefaction' or tensile effect and leading to cavitation and/or tearing.

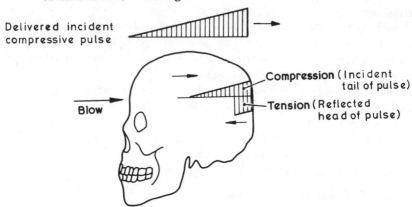

Fig. 28. Incident and reflected pulses in the skull due to a blow; the blow is assumed to reflect from the far side of the brain as if it was a free surface

(b) Compressive pulses delivered at a pole, or induced at the site of the blow or 'coup', may be reflected as tensile or rarefaction pulses at an anti-pole and cause a counter-blow or 'contre-coup'. Hence there may be 'proximal' damage at the initiating location due directly to the blow, or there may be 'distal' damage due to the counter-blow. This is to say that a blow on one side of the head may cause an injury on the opposite side. (As remarked above, the latter may only be recognized to have happened when certain mental or physical processes which are localized in the brain are medically observed in dysfunction.)

2. Two simultaneous causes† of brain damage can be

† The 'punch-drunk' boxer is a well known example of the consequences of brain injury, probably due to repeated blows; the condition tends to be one of progressive deterioration. The light-weight boxer (36) is most prone to suffer punch-drunkness. The introduction and use of boxing gloves, as against unprotected bare fists, is said to have changed the nature of the head damage inflicted in boxing, but is imperfectly understood. Probably the most comprehensive review of head injuries in sport is that by Unterharnscheidt (46).

(a) skull deformation due to local depression, indentation or vibration of parts of the skull, with or without fracture, and,
(b) rotational acceleration of the head due to a tangential blow – e.g., a 'hook' or 'upper-cut' – leading to relative angular motion between the skull and the fluid-like brain, thus introducing significant shear strain between them, with tearing of the connected structures.

It is often maintained that for blows delivered between 2 and 200 ms, brain damage is controlled by impulse, but for larger times by force.

    3.   Flexion-extension and/or bending of the upper cervical cord during motion of the head–neck junction; this is whip-lash injury.

An elementary expression for cavitation damage due to a blow
Several investigators have endeavoured to consider head impact in terms of elementary engineering elastic stress wave theory, as applied to a long bar. If the theory associated with the notion of spalling, see Fig. 29 and ref. **(4)** is used, the blow being conceived of as compressive and triangular in shape, and the bar being identified with the brain, then after reflection at a supposedly free end, the tensile stress generated is first greatest at $l/2$ from the distal end and its magnitude is $\sigma_0 = \rho c v$; the corresponding speed of the particles is $\sigma_0/\rho c$, where ρ denotes the density of brain substance and $c = 150$ m/s is the speed of pressure waves in it. The stress σ_0 is the amount by which the pressure in the contre-coup region is reduced. If the limit to this is p_c, the cavitation pressure, (dissolved gases come out of solution in liquids and voids form at this pressure), then the speed of a blow at which cavitation occurs is $v = p_c/\rho c$. For the quantities specified, and as $\rho \simeq 1$ g/cm^3 and $p_c = 12$ N/cm^2, $v \simeq 80$ cm/s or 3 ft/s.
    The approach here is greatly over simplified but it does convey some useful notions.

Obtaining information
To obtain information about body behaviour, and particularly to measure retardation rates or pulses to which various parts or points on the human body are subjected under collision conditions, it is usual to use volunteer human beings, cadavers, anthropomorphic dummies or live animals (especially monkeys). Dummies have only recently come to be able to be modelled in such a sufficiently sophisticated way as to render them reliable material. When a human volunteer is not available or cannot be

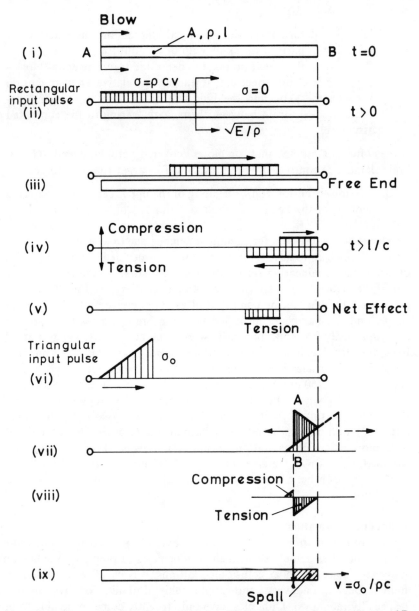

Fig. 29. *Incident and reflected pulses in a bar. If the net tension in a section, e.g.,* AB *exceeds the tensile fracture stress of the bar, the end portion flies off at speed v as a spall*

used, the cadaver (or dummy) is usually employed but it will not of course respond precisely as would a living person.

Instrumented cadavers and dummies, probably restrained by a belt and shoulder strap, are seated in cars for impact tests or mounted in sleds for investigation at controlled rates of acceleration. Figure 30(a) shows an early (1967) set of readings pertaining to a cadaver mounted in a sled, and Fig. 30(b) is a set obtained for volunteers; the magnification of the magnitude of retardation from seat to head should be noted.

Colonel Stapp (USA) was a pioneer volunteer in testing; investigations of this type, and many research results in this area of work, are published through the Stapp Car Crash Conferences (1); see also the work by Perrone (37) on biomechanical problems related to vehicle impact.

Sophisticated, up-to-date computer code references and details about crash victim simulation are available (38).

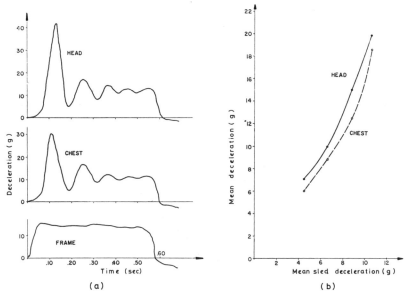

Fig. 30. (a) *Decelerations in a simulated impact;* (b) *Mean head and chest decelerations from volunteer tests*

Gadd Severity Index

A curve proposed by Lissner *et al.*, in 1960 and modified by Patrick *et al.*, became the Wayne State Tolerance Curve widely used in automobile safety research (Fig. 31). It claims to define the level at which acceleration,

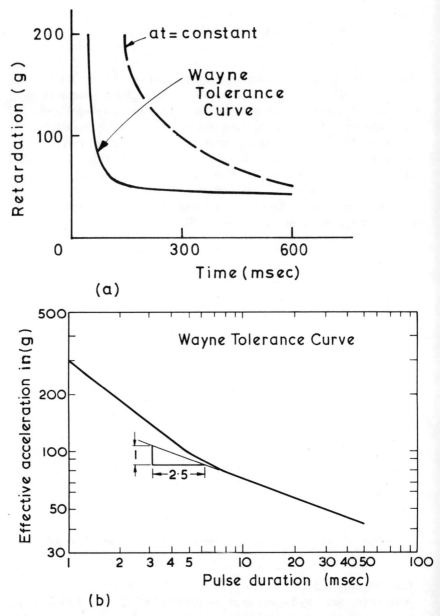

Fig. 31. *Gadd Severity Index:* (a) *Retardation–time diagram;* (b) *Wayne Tolerance Curve for head impact*

or retardation, of the head causes concussion and skull fracture. It is based on an average acceleration of the skull (a square pulse) at the occipital bone for impacts of the forehead against a plane, unyielding surface.

The Wayne curve is the basis of several indices of injury severity, the most popular index being that due to Gadd. A single number is identified to represent tolerance for various regions of the body. It is very helpful to safety design engineers to have to satisfy a specified numerical requirement. For the head, the Gadd Severity Index is

$$\int_0^T a^{2\cdot5}\mathrm{d}t$$

where a is acceleration expressed in terms of the number of g, t is time, and T the pulse length, in milliseconds.

A value of 1000 is taken as the threshold for serious internal head injury for frontal impact; this purports to identify the level that could be tolerated without permanent brain damage or skull fracture being incurred for a normal healthy adult.

The index $2\cdot5$ is primarily a straight line approximation to the Wayne State Tolerance Curve, between $2\cdot5$ and 50 milliseconds.

Recent work on skull fracture (1970) tends to validate (as far as one number can) the use of this Index and it was accepted by the Society of Automobile Engineers about 1966.†

The criterion for avoiding fatality is then:

$$\int_0^T a^{2\cdot5}\mathrm{d}t < 1000;$$

the pulse time T must be such that $0\cdot25$ ms $< T <$ 50 ms.

If a rigidly seated driver, who is restrained by a seat belt, was brought

† In 1972 Gadd proposed that a level of 1500 be adopted for distributed impact. For some purposes the Gadd S.I. has been superseded by the Head Impact Criterion,

$$\text{H.I.C.} = \max \ (t_2 - t_1)\left(\frac{1}{t_2 - t_1}\int_{t_1}^{t_2} a(t)\mathrm{d}t\right)^{2.5} < 1000,$$

where t_1 and t_2 are the initial and final time during the pulse for which the H.I.C. attains a maximum value; $a(t)$ is the resultant acceleration and $\mathrm{d}t$ the time increment.

to rest from speed v with uniform acceleration in a distance s, the Gadd Severity Index would be given by

$$G.S.I. = \frac{v^4/g}{(2sg)^{1 \cdot 5}}.$$

If the frontal crushing distance of a car is $0 \cdot 6$ m (2 ft) and s is equated to this, the speed required to attain the tolerance limit would be 92 km/h (57 miles/h). Note, however, that 'no serious head or neck injury has been seen without direct contact . . . For the (belt) restrained driver, face contact with the wheel is the rule . . .' (39). A 'car occupant wearing a 3-point lap and diagonal safety belt . . . suffers concussion . . . (as a) result of impact of the head with the inside of the car' (40).

Thoracic and abdominal injury criteria
Results gained from work on volunteers and cadavers, and through accident studies, lead to the belief that *rib* fracture occurs for distributed loads of between $5 \cdot 3$ kN (1200 lbf) and $8 \cdot 9$ kN (2000 lbf). Rupture of the great vessels in the thoracic cage sometimes occurs but volunteer tests suggest that 60 g for up to 100 ms can be tolerated.

Load distribution over the chest is important. For British cars it is claimed that axial steering column collapse systems are ineffective in limiting chest loads.

Lower limbs
The knee, femur and pelvis skeletal complex is injured in 40 per cent of seriously injured front seat car occupants. It has been suggested that $6 \cdot 2$ kN (1400 lbf) is the appropriate tolerance level for the femur. It is, however, also thought to be too high and, furthermore, that traumatic fracture is not the appropriate criterion but rather post-traumatic arthritis of the knee and pelvic joints; this may only occur, however, long after the accident.

It is noteworthy that in the UK, 68 per cent of front seat passengers are female and 83 per cent are male. Thus different injury criteria might be appropriate for the two front seat positions.

An alternative criterion which has been specified for the chest and pelvis is that they should not have to endure 60 g for more than 3 ms.

Aside from other references given in this review the treatment of impact insensitivity for structures and for animals and men by Kornhauser (41) is important and useful.

56

CRASH HELMETS

A maximum peak force of 19·6 kN (4400 lbf) acting on the skull is used as a design criterion for crash helmets; it represents the force required to fracture the average cadaver skull when acting through the scalp on an area of about 13 cm² (2 in²) as Gurdjian *et al.* (**42**), determined from experiments by dropping cadaver skulls on to hard flat surfaces. However, live skulls are believed to perform better than those of cadavers. A good measure of local protection is afforded by a stiff helmet with suitable load-spreading and energy absorbent liners when the impact energy reaches 168 to 204 Nm (120 to 150 lbf ft).

Angular acceleration is a chief cause of injury and death, but little can be done to prevent this because of the difficulty of arresting rotational movement with a helmet of practicable design, and because the brain mass (inertia) responds slowly to changes of speed. Much the same applies concerning translational motion.

Helmets should be made penetration resistant, smooth, and spherical enough to deflect a high proportion of blows to the head. The whole assembly should, however, have a low coefficient of restitution ($e < 0·3$) so that change of head speed is minimized.

Crash helmets seem to function mainly by reducing the danger of skull fracture and this is best achieved by spreading the impact load. Stiff liners make for high rise, short time intervals and hence large uncomfortable forces on the skull. Low rated liners allow large displacements and too little velocity reduction before 'bottoming' occurs with consequent very high forces on the skull. The need for compromise is evident. See also the recent work by Simpson *et al.* (**43**), on the impact of a head-helmet system.

American interest in this topic was recently stimulated when revising helmet design, in the light of military casualties resulting from shrapnel impact (**38**). See also ref. (**44**) and the article by Johnson and Teanor (**45**) in which the reasons for the kind of impact protections adopted by the US Army aviator helmets are listed.

REFERENCES

(1) Proc. 20th Stapp Car Crash Conference 1976, Amer. Soc. Auto. Engrs.
(2) PUGSLEY, A. G., *The Safety of Structures* 1966, (Arnold, London).
(3) NADER, R., *Unsafe at Any Speed* 1973, (Bantam, London).

(4) JOHNSON, W., and MAMALIS, A. G., 'Gegenüberstellung statischer und dynamischer Schadens oder Deformationserscheinungen', *Fortschr. - Ber.* VDI-Z., 1977, Reihe 5, No. 32.

(5) FRANCHINI, E., 'The Crash Survival Space', 1969, Soc. Auto. Engrs, 690005.

(6) GRIME, G., and JONES, I. S., 'Car Collisions - The Movement of Cars and their Occupants in Accidents', 1970, Inst. Mech. Engrs, Automobile Division, AD P5/70.

(7) WOJCIK, C. K., and HULBERT, S. F., 'Inertia Forces in Driving and their Simulation', 1967, *Trans. ASME*, Paper 66-WA/BHF-11.

(8) RAWLINGS, B., 'Response of Structures to Dynamic Loads', Conf. on Mechanical Properties at High Rates of Strain, 1974, Inst. of Physics, Oxford, 279.

(9) SODEN, P. D., AL-HASSANI, S. T. S., and JOHNSON, W., 'The Crumpling of Polyvinylchloride Tubes under Static and Dynamic Axial Loads', 1974, Inst. of Physics Conf., Series Nr. 21, Oxford, 327.

(10) ABRAHAMSON, G. R., and GOODIER, J. N., 'Dynamic Flexural Buckling of Rods within an Axial Plastic Compression Wave', *J. App. Mech.*, 1966, **33**, 241.

(11) MACAULAY, M. A., and REDWOOD, R. G., 'Small Scale Model Railway Coaches under Impact', *The Engineer*, 1964, **218**, 1041.

(12) REDWOOD, R. G., 'On the Buckling of Thin Walled Tubes under Axial Impact', *J. Roy. Aero. Soc.*, 1964, **68**, 418.

(13) COPPA, A. P., 'The Buckling of Circular Cylindrical Shells Subject to Axial Impact', 1962, NASA Tech. Note D-1510.

(14) EDWARDS, A. M., 'The Effects of Plasticity on the Buckling and Post-Buckling of Circular Cylindrical Shells', 1965, Stanford University Ph.D Thesis.

(15) HORTON, W. H., BAILEY, S. C., and EDWARDS, A. M., 'Non-Symmetric Buckle Pattern in Progressive Plastic Buckling', *Experimental Mechanics*, 1966, **6**, 433.

(16) POSTLETHWAITE, H. E., and MILLS B., 'Use of Collapsible Structural Elements as Impact Isolators with Special Reference to Automotive Applications', *J. Strain Analysis*, 1970, **5**, 58.

(17) NI, C. M., 'Impact Response of Curved Box-Beam Columns', 14th Structural Conference, 1973, AIAA/ASME/SAE, AIAA Paper No. 73-401.

(18) MILES, J. C., 'The Determination of Collapse Load and Energy Absorbing Properties of Thin Walled Beam Structures Using Matrix Methods of Analysis', *Int. J. Mech. Sci.*, 1976, **18**, 399.

(19) NAGY, L. I., *Finite Element Method of Automobile Design, Theory and Practice in Finite Element Structural Design*, 1973, (Univ. of Tokyo Press).

(20) MCIVOR, I. K., ANDERSON, W. J., and BIJAK-ZOCHOWSKI, M., 'An Experimental Study of the Large Deformation of Plastic Hinges', *Int. J. Sol. Struct.*, 1977, **13**, 53.

(21) MCIVOR, I. K., WINEMAN, A. S., and WANG, H. C., 'Plastic Collapse of General Frames', *Int. J. Sol. Struct.*, 1977, **13**, 197.

(22) BARACES, W., and RHODES, A., 'Ford "S"-Frame', 1969, Soc. Auto. Engrs., 690004.

(23) WIRSCHING, R. H., and SLATER, R. C., 'The Beer Can as a Shock Absorber', *Trans. ASME, J. Eng. Mater. Tech.*, 1973, **H95**, 224.

(24) 'Symposium on Car Safety Design', London, *Proc. Inst. Mech. Engrs*, 1968–9, **183**, (Part 3A), p. 25.

(25) MACMILLAN, R. H., 'Primary Safety: Vehicle Design to Avoid Accidents', *Proc. Inst. Mech. Engrs*, 1972, **186**, 479.

(26) MACKAY, G. M., 'The Effectiveness of Vehicle Safety Design Changes in Accident and Injury Reduction', Conf. Vehicle Safety Legislations, Inst. Mech. Engrs, (July 1973).

58

(27) COOMBS, B., 'Safety Frames for Tractors', *Farm Machine Design, Engineering Supplement*, Dec. 1971, 59.

(28) EMORI, R. I., 'Scale Models of Automobile Collisions with Breakaway Obstacles', *Experimental Mechanics*, 1973, **13**, 64.

(29) HOLMES, B. S., and SLITER, G., 'Scale Modelling of Vehicle Coaches', 1974, Soc. Auto. Engrs, 740586.

(30) HOLMES, B. S., and COLTON, J. D., 'Scale Model Experiments for Safety Car Development', 1973, Soc. Auto. Engrs, 730073.

(31) SNYDER, R. G., 'Evaluation of Inflatable (Air Bag) Occupant Restraint Systems for Aircraft Application', *SAFE Journal*, 1977, **7**, (3), 16.

(32) LOWE, W. T., AL-HASSANI, S. T. S., and JOHNSON, W., 'Impact Behaviour of Small Scale Model Motor Coaches', *Proc. Inst. Mech. Engrs*, 1972, **186**, 409.

(33) WESTCOTT, J. S., 'Safety Motor Cycle', *Proc. Inst. Mech. Engrs*, 1975, **189**, 1.

(34) 'Frontal Barrier Impact of an Invacar Model 70 Tricycle', 1973, MIRA, Project No. KO45.

(35) HOLBOURN, A. H. S., 'Mechanics of Head Iniuries' *The Lancet*. 1943. 438.

(36) JOHNSON, J., 'Organic Psychosyndromes Due to Boxing', *Brit. J. Psychiatry*, 1969, **115**, 45.

(37) PERRONE, N., 'Biomechanical Problems Related to Vehicle Impact', *Biomechanics: Its Foundations and Objectives*, Ed. FUNG, Y. C., *et al.*, 1972 (Prentice-Hall Inc.).

(38) HUSTON, R. L., *Three-Dimensional Crash-Motion Crash Simulation*, Structural Mechanics Software Series, Vol. 1, Ed. PERRONE, N., PILKEY, W., and PILKEY, B., 1977, 615, (Univ. Press of Virginia).

(39) MACKAY, G. M., *et al.*, 'Serious Trauma to Car Occupants Wearing Seat Belts', 2nd Int. Conf. Biomechanics of Serious Trauma, (Sept. 1975).

(40) GRIME, G., 'Head and Neck Injuries to Car Occupants Wearing Seat Belts in Frontal Collisions', *Ibid*, p. 30.

(41) KORNHAUSER, M., *Structural Effects of Impact*, 1964, (Cleaver-Hume Press Ltd, London).

(42) RAYNE, J. M., 'Dynamic Behaviour of Crash Helmets', 1969, RAE Tech. Report, 69/60 – ARC 31726.

(43) SIMPSON, B. A., GOLDSMITH, W., and SACKMAN, J. L., 'Oblique Impact on a Head-Helmet System', *Int. J. Mech. Sci.*, 1976, **18**, 337.

(44) HODGSON, V. R., 'Head Injury Criteria and Evaluation of Protective Head Gear', in *Measurement and Prediction of Structural and Biodynamic Crash-Impact Response*, Eds SACZALSKI, K. J., and PILKEY, W. D., ASME Conference, (December 1976), 121.

(45) JOHNSON, G. L., and TREANOR, J. J., 'The Helmet Protects the Aviator's Head – or Does it?', *SAFE Journal*, 1977, **7**, (3), 20.

(46) UNTERHARNSCHEIDT, F. J., 'Injuries Due to Boxing and Other Sports', *Handbook of Clinical Neurology*, Ch. 26, Vol. 23, pp. 525–93, 1975 (North Holland Publishing Co.).

Part II: Severe damage to rolling stock

'It may be argued that the level of safety on the railways is higher than can be justified economically.'†

I. K. A. McNaughton
Chief Inspecting Officer of Railways,
15th Sir Seymour Biscoe Tritton Lecture, Inst. Civil Engrs, London, 1976 **(1)**

Aspects of locomotive and truck mechanics

Two categories of severe damage to railway rolling stock may be identified: (1) that arising principally from end-collisions and (2) that due to derailments; high speed end-collision usually ends in derailment,‡ see Fig. 32. The circumstances of relatively infrequent derailment are so various that only the most general observations about its mechanics, and any passive§ safety features can be positively considered. The slow speed end-collision of wagons and coaches has of course long been the subject of some rational design and experimental testing, leading to braking¶ and buffing systems.

The detailed design of buffers is a subject of historical standing and one well treated in, for instance ref. **(1)**.

Some simple, basic mechanics as between colliding wagons is given by Inglis **(3)** and the following interesting results are taken from his book.

---

† It is estimated that the road rate of accident is ten times higher than on the railways.
‡ Duncan *et al.* **(18)** consider the principal cause to be flange climb; physical lifting clear of the rail is mentioned to result from 'longitudinal shocks in the train' and a figure is shown of heavily laden wagons being 'squeezed up' during braking trials.
§ Track super-elevation would be an active safety feature.
¶ Bond and Nock **(2)** note that, 'Engineers refused to fit any form of brakes on their locomotives because it was feared that application of retarding forces to the wheels would strain the machinery. All that was done was to put hand-operated brakes on to the wheels of the tender. On passenger trains there were two "brake vans", one at the front and one at the rear. There was a recognized code whereby the driver whistled for the brakes to be applied. The guards in the front and rear vans applied them by hand, and apart from this an express passenger train of the late 1860s, often travelling at more than 60 miles per hour, was entirely devoid of brakes! Several disastrous accidents, accompanied by grievous loss of life, highlighted the shortcomings both in brake power, and in methods of traffic regulation.'

Fig. 32. High speed end-collision usually ends in derailment

(1) If identical wagons moving with the same speed u, collide at O as in Fig. 33(a), when the compression of the buffers is greatest, the contact point O moves vertically upward with a speed of v, given by

$$v = \frac{dh}{a^2 + k^2 + h^2} \cdot u,$$

if the trucks are without springs and if the inertia of the wheels is neglected; k is the radius of gyration of each truck about a transverse horizontal axis through its centre of gravity, G. Note that I in Fig. 33(a) is the instantaneous centre of rotation of each truck and the angular velocity of each about it is v/d.

(2) If, however, in the last case the truck is spring-borne, the vertical shock generated at A will not now be produced to give G a vertical speed. Truck rotation ω about G must thus be about a point on the vertical line through G; hence $\omega = v/(a + d)$. Again applying the principles of moment of momentum (on a horizontal line through O) leads to

$$v/u = h\,(a + d)/(h^2 + k^2) \text{ and } \omega/u = h/(h^2 + k^2).$$

(3) In the case of dissimilar trucks, see Fig. 33(b), with B stationary and A moving to the left at speed U, when the buffer springs are fully compressed

61

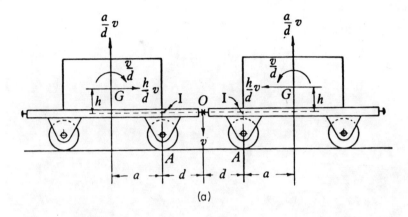

(a)

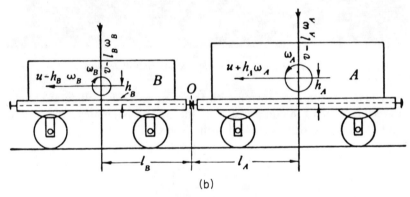

(b)

Fig. 33. Head-on collision of two trucks (a) similar, (b) dissimilar

the angular velocities are found to be – since the moment of momentum of A and B about O are unchanged –

$$\omega_A = \frac{l_A v - h_A \cdot u + h_A U_A}{l_A^2 + k_A^2 + h_A^2} \quad \text{and} \quad \omega_B = \frac{l_B v + h_B u}{l_B^2 + k_B^2 + h_B^2}.$$

Since the total horizontal and vertical momenta are unchanged

$$(M_A + M_B)u + M_A h_A \omega_A - M_B h_B \omega_B = M_A U,$$

and $(M_A + M_B)v - M_A l_A \omega_A - M_B l_B \omega_B = 0.$

The last four equations now enable u, v, ω_A and ω_B to be found.

62

Calculations (4) for a railway rolling wheel suddenly striking a possible small rigid step show that (typically) the wheel acceleration could well be 540 g and the (unacceptable) truck load created would be 20 times normal wheel-rail load; the consequences would be too great for the normal range of truck and suspension stiffnesses.

Railroad coaches (4) in the USA specify that the axial strength of cars, i.e., loads at which permanent deformation of any member is not developed in the unit for inter-city service are 2200 kN (500 000 lbf). Transit cars for the Washington Metro have a strength of 890 kN (200 000 lbf) and 'zero permanent deformation' strength for most cars lies in the range 890–1780 kN (2–400 000 lbf). The strength for significant structural collapse is thought to be twice this value. The maximum permissible retardation of a conventional ten-car US commuter train of weight $6\cdot4 \times 10^4$ kg per car and estimated collapse load 7200 kN, is $1\cdot1$ g.

For unrestrained standing passengers, the tolerable retardation rate appears to be between 1 and 2 g so that with plastic deformation energy absorbers, the required stroke length s is approximately given by the kinetic energy to be absorbed divided by the permissible crushing load; for a fixed 1 g retardation rate, $s = v^2/2g$ and if $v = 40$ km/h, $s \simeq 6\cdot4$ m. Such a stroke length is impracticably large for an energy absorbing device fixed at the end of any coach.

Lateral as well as vertical motion occurs in head-on collisions, see p. 17, and anti-climbing devices and crash posts are often not sufficient protection against it.

Because of their massiveness, it is to be observed that locomotives can withstand greater axial loads than coaches and thus in any collision, the latter will undergo plastic deformation before or to a more significant degree than the former.† Further, destructive action at the point of impact begins before the buffers between any first and second coaches are completely compressed and the distance covered by a coach during retardation increases with distance from the point of impact. It is supposed by some that the mean value of the forces transmitted between individual coaches reduces linearly towards the rear of the train.

Of the four cases of locomotive and coach collision illustrated in Fig. 34, case (b) would be most disastrous because larger forces would be generated at impact by the stiffer bodies than in the other cases and thus greater

---

† The same applies when comparing heavy lorries and cars; and that the height of the bumper and body above the ground for a lorry is greater than that of a car is also partly responsible for the disastrous effect of the former on the latter.

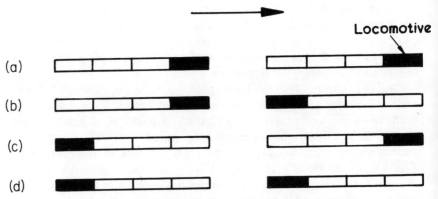

Fig. 34. *Illustrating locomotive and coach collision situations*

retardation rates would be created. In high speed collisions, front vehicles derail almost without exception.

It has been observed **(5)** that:

(a) In a train, coaches which are of reduced compressive strength, are particularly dangerous because in any deforming situation they may cause other coaches to turn and telescope.

(b) The height of centres of gravity should be low to lessen turning moment magnitudes and thus the tendency for coaches to climb one onto the other.

(c) Long coaches, due to their increased weight, oppose any turning moment better than do short coaches.

(d) Front-end vertical structural members and their connections with the roof should be as strong as possible; the greatest degree of plastic deformation occurs in the region through which impact first occurs, see Fig. 39.

(e) Buffers that incorporate a destructible element that enables them to be pushed-in when a pre-selected force is exceeded are advisable so that front ends come into contact over an entire surface.

There seems to be virtually nothing written about side impact as between coaches or between a locomotive and coaches. Because of the greater mass of a (single-frame) locomotive, the upper edge of its rigid frame is likely to tear away the relatively 'soft' side of a coach above its longitudinal members and to cause damage deeper into the coach than into the locomotive. Derailed leading locomotives dig heavily into a track

64

or ballast and usually come to a standstill in a short distance; this implies very high retardation rates with consequent heavy damage in following coaches.

Tank wagons

The first tank wagons in the UK were built about 1865 (6) to carry tar from gas-works to chemical plants and were D-shaped barrels attached to a wooden underframe. By 1881 a half-round barrel had been introduced which, to accommodate increased train speeds and buffing-forces, was held down to the underframe by straps and heavy wooden stanchions. In 1965, wagons of 100-ton gross laden weight were introduced to carry petrol and the like and the design considerations concerning such wagons are discussed at length by Smith (6). Aside from other features, for countering dynamic loading, metallic tank barrels are today attached to the wagon underframe; in the fully laden condition they must be capable of withstanding a minimum force of four times their total laden weight in the direction of travel, as well as their own weight transverse to the travel direction and vertically upwards, and twice their weight vertically downwards.

Liquid surge loading and buffing shocks especially have to be considered in tank wagon design.† Large vertical transverse plates (and 'half' baffle plates) inside barrels have been incorporated to reduce surge forces, but when surge occurs it leads to stress problems at the baffle plate attachment. As a result of tests it was recommended that tank wagons without baffles were safe and hence they were recommended to be removed and are not included in new wagons (6).

Auxiliary explosive hazards arise when the free space remaining in a tank after loading (ullage) is insufficient to allow for expansion of a product after an increase in temperature.

The consequences of catastrophic venting, i.e., tank or head puncturing (7) has become very important in recent years with the rail transportation of hazardous materials; such may result from collisions, flying fragments or fire. The knuckle radius is more susceptible to impact damage than the tank head centre. The puncturing of sheet by sharp-end metal objects is discussed in ref. (17).

† See *Proc. Sixth Int. Ship Structures Conference, Vol. I*, Committee Report 113, 1976, p. 31.

The Moorgate tube disaster: Pile-up in a tunnel (8)

At the Moorgate Underground Tube Station, London, on 28 February 1975, 43 persons were killed when a train of two 3-car units, length 96 m (316 ft) and weight above 1500 kN (150 tons), overran its platform and travelled into an overrun tunnel of length 20 m (67 ft) at about 16·1 m/s (53 ft/s). It dispersed the sand-drag – a cheap and sometimes effective method of bringing an external retarding force to bear – and demolished a single central hydraulic buffer stop at the end of the tunnel. The leading car reared up so that the driver's cab impinged against the tunnel wall close to the top of the 4·9 m (16 ft) high tunnel (Fig. 35). The underframe buckled into three sections, with its rear end crushed into the roof; the 15·8 m (52 ft) long coach was crushed into 6 m (20 ft) of tunnel. The second car was driven forward beneath the rear end of the leading car; its body-work at the leading end was heavily crushed. The rear end of the second car was crushed having been over-ridden by the leading end of the third coach (Fig. 36). This third car was relatively undamaged except at the leading end. The fourth car was slightly damaged but not the fifth and sixth ones.

The underframe of these coaches required a load of about 500 kN (50 tons) to cause it to undergo plastic deformation. The sand-drag was heaped 0·6 m (2 ft) above rail level (about one half axle height), was 7·9 m (26 ft) long and weighed about 200 kN (20 tons)† (Fig. 37). The bogie of the leading coach was presumed to have dispersed the sand which is thought only to have reduced the speed of impact with the buffer from 16·1 to 15·2 m/s (53 to 50 ft/s).

The leading end of the third coach ended at about 15·2 m (50 ft) from the buffer, see Fig. 37, so that the rear four coaches were retarded over a distance of (150–100) ft or at an average rate of $50^2/2 \times 50 \simeq 7\cdot6$ m/s² (25 ft/s²). The mean retardation force was thus $(150 \times 4/6) (25/g) \simeq 800$ kN (80 tons). The leading end of the second coach stopped at 4 m (13 ft) from the tunnel end and hence in a distance of 11·3 m (37 ft); the mean retardation rate was thus about 10·4 m/s (34 ft/s) and the mean retardation force approximately $(150 \times 5/6) (34/32) \simeq 1250$ kN (125 tons).

A comment that is interesting and useful for designers was made by a survivor from a crumpled carriage. 'We were sitting near the middle of the carriage close to the central doors and the door arches strengthened the roof and formed a sort of tent which probably saved us. On either side

† Friction buffer stops which slide back along the rails and similar retarders are not able to withstand initial impact speeds of more than 9·1 m/s (30 ft/s).

66

Fig. 35. Showing degree of crushing of coach in the tunnel (*Photo by Press Association: The Daily Telegraph, 1 March 1975*)

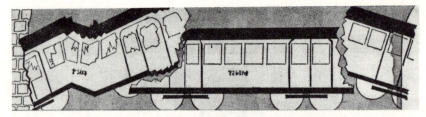

Fig. 36. Sketch of buckling and crushing of first three coaches

the roof had been squashed to the floor.' The notion of a strengthened shell or capsule is evident here; compare the remarks about it in cars, p. 31 and the necessity for it in light aircraft design, p. 87.

For a subway car of 102 kN (23 000 lbf) weight (as opposed to a subway train of several coaches) which overshoots its unloading platform at up to 7·6 m/s (25 ft/s), Kirk (9) has designed (using an idea due to Shaw) a metal-skinning device which would absorb uniformly, the kinetic energy of the car and bring it to rest at an acceptable rate of about 1 *g* in 6·1 m (20 ft). Essentially, during overshoot a circular bar is pulled through a cutting tool so that the tool machines off the outer layer of several aluminium rods (Fig. 38), thereby dissipating kinetic energy. Collision tests have verified the worth of the design which is intended for the US Capitol Subway System.

Model tests
Tests on model railway coaches subjected to end-impact are reported in ref. (10); note from Fig. 39 how the most serious damage (plastic deformation) is concentrated over a distance equal to about the transverse width or height of the coach at the impact end.

The model testing principles described on p. 32 should be kept in mind.

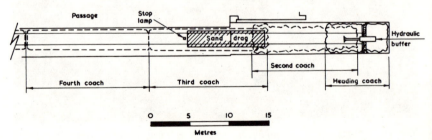

Fig. 37. Showing position in which train came to rest at Moorgate

68

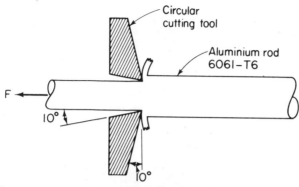

Fig. 38. Schematic diagram of a metal skinning device

Fig. 39. Damaged coach model due to end impact

Train arrester beds†

1. *Foam* (**11**)

Urea formaldehyde foam is a non-flammable plastic that can be laid in a retaining structure in the ground by pumping from a hose-pipe. After special mixing and a rapid curing, this gives a rigid cell structure somewhat similar to compact snow. A vehicle which runs on to a bed of foam

† But see also pp. 81–87.

crushes it, and experiences a drag on impact which brings it to rest in an acceptable distance so that its kinetic energy is dissipated (11). The density of the material is controllable so that vehicle retardation rates are, to some degree, controllable also. The British Rail Advanced Passenger train (of 117 tons weight and maximum speed 250 km/h) was tested using foam-arrester beds; during trials, a 66-ton locomotive was run into the foam at speeds of up to 96 km/h and was arrested with little damage to the structure or wheels and bogies.

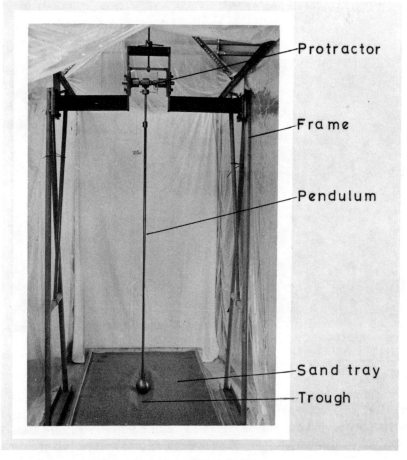

Fig. 40. (a) *A pendulum bob apparatus for studying energy loss* versus *crater volume*

70

2. Sand

The employment of sand, as in the sand-drag for arresting trains (and retarding them by using a sand-box for braking and thus increasing adhesion) is of long standing; however, there is no rational theory of sand dynamics available for use in design situations. Sand penetration by high speed projectiles and their ricochetting behaviour off sand is discussed in refs (12) and (13). Low speed superficial ploughing of sand can be usefully investigated with reference to energy dissipation by allowing a heavy pendulum bob to swing into a sand box, see Fig. 40(a), to determine energy versus crater volume curves, and sand dispersal profiles (14); Fig. 40(b) shows a typical plough, made by a solid metal pendulum bob, in a sand box of narrow width. This same pendulum system may be used to study the spillage of material from an open-top container. Figure 40(c) indicates how a mass of sand (into which a rectangular grid of a light coloured sand was first introduced) has moved when the moving front of the container was suddenly arrested.†

The stress distribution and thence centre of pressure due to the impact of say, free-running sand against an inclined surface, is likely to be best estimated by reference to results for the impact of a non-viscous liquid jet on an inclined plate (15, 16) rather than by use of the principles of hydrostatics.

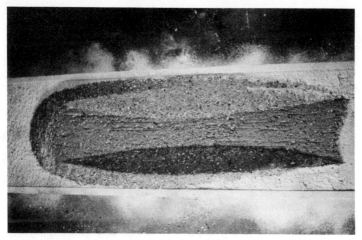

Fig. 40.(b) *The crater caused in a narrow box by a swinging spherical bob*

† In the paper by Duncan *et al.* (18) examples are shown of cargo shift during transportation and bad initial loading in railway wagons, which promoted derailment.

Fig. 40. (c) *Sand spillage; movement and heaping after the frontal impact of a full rectangular container. The grid of light coloured sand was initially rectangular*

REFERENCES

(1) MCNAUGHTON, I. K. A., 15th Sir Seymour Biscoe Tritton Lecture, 1976, Inst. Civil Engrs, London.
(2) BOND, R. C., and NOCK, O. S., '150 Years of Uninterrupted Progress in Railway Engineering', *Proc. Inst. Mech. Engrs*, 1975, **189**, 589.
(3) INGLIS, C. E., *Applied Mechanics for Engineers*, 1951, (C.U.P., Cambridge).
(4) NEWLAND, D. E., and CASSIDY, R. J., 'Suspension and Structure: Some Fundamental Design Considerations for Railway Vehicles', *Railway Engr. J.*, 1975, **4**, 4.
(5) Notes Supplied by Swiss Federal Railways, 18 Jan. 1963; Private Communication via Col. I. K. A., MCNAUGHTON, 1975.
(6) SMITH, A. D., 'Tank Wagons for the Conveyance of Dangerous Goods on B.R. Lines', *Railway Engr. J.*, 1974, **3**, 2.
(7) SHANG, J. C., and EVERETT, J. E., 'Impact Vulnerability of Tank Car Heads', *Shock and Vibration Bulletin Naval Res. Lab.*, 1972, **42**, 197.
(8) *Railway Accident Report on the Accident that Occurred on 28 February 1975 at Moorgate Station*, (HMSO, London).
(9) KIRK, J. A., 'Design of a Metal Skinning Energy Absorber for the U.S. Capitol Subway System', *Int. J. Mech. Sci.*, 1977, **19**, 595.
(10) MACAULAY, M. A., and REDWOOD, R. G., 'Small Scale Model Railway Coaches under Impact', *The Engineer*, 1964, **218**, 1041.
(11) 'Beetle', Urea Formaldehyde Foam, Attachment 'C'.
(12) ALLEN, W. A., MAYFIELD, E. B., and MORRISON, H. L., 'Dynamics of a Projectile Penetrating Sand', *J. Appl. Physics*, 1957, **28**, 370.

(13) SOLIMAN, S. F., REID, S. R., and JOHNSON, W., 'The Effect of Spherical Projectile Speed in Ricochet off Water and Sand', *Int. J. Mech. Sci.*, 1976, **18**, 279.
(14) JOHNSON, W., CLYENS, S., and GUPTA, N. (To be published).
(15) BATCHELOR, G. K., *Fluid Dynamics*, 1970, (C.U.P., Cambridge).
(16) RAYLEIGH, Lord, 'On the Resistance of Fluids', *Phil. Mag.*, 1876, **2**, 430.
(17) JOHNSON, W., CHITKARA, N. R., and BEX, P. A., 'Characteristic Features in the Hole Flanging and Piercing of Thin and Thick Circular Plates Using Conical and Ogival Punches', 1974, 15th Int. M.T.D.R. Conference, Birmingham, 695.
(18) DUNCAN, I. G. T., McCANN, J. B. C., and BROWN, A., 'The Investigations of Derailments', *Proc. Inst. Mech. Engrs*, 1977, **191**, 323.

Part III: Aircraft impact

A large amount of effort, especially in the USA, is now being devoted to studies of aircraft impact with the very clear aim of facilitating design for reducing damage to the aircraft itself – a very expensive item – and its contents, i.e., passengers and cargo. In aircraft accidents, a much larger fraction of those involved are usually killed or seriously injured than is the case with other vehicles, usually because of the relative lightness of the vehicle itself and the magnitude of the operating speeds.

Accidents
Accident investigation procedures, experience, and records are outlined in refs **(1)**, **(2)**, **(3)** and **(4)** but they are not of direct interest here, where we are concerned with collision processes and not their cause.† It seems that only recently have aircraft impact processes become the object of deliberate experiment and study; previously, aims have been wholly to improve reliability and scarcely to consider the accident process itself. When an accident has occurred, though the protection of passengers is what matters most, the tendency has been to view the situation as totally beyond control.

Wreckage trails, following aircraft mid-air break-up, are generally discussed in ref. **(1)**, and ref. **(5)** repeats an analysis by Mandl and Givens, originally produced to try to ascertain the speed and inclination at impact at which an aircraft crashed into clay, from the depth of burial of the wreckage fragments. Penetration into sand is also treated in refs **(5)** and **(12)** of the previous Part; see page 72.

Aside from the wide personal experiences of ref. **(1)** a very careful and useful post-crash study was made of a turbojet ditching **(6)**. A critical review was carried out of the ditching of a DC-9 aircraft in May 1970 in the Caribbean Sea when 23 out of 63 persons lost their lives. At impact with the water, the aircraft floor structure was said to be subjected to a vertical retardation of 8 to 12 g for 0·5 to 1·0 s and the plane to have been brought to a halt in 15 to 24 m, after the fuselage had become immersed in the water; the occupiable areas of the aircraft were thought not to have been compromised.

---

† The book *Destination Disaster* **(22)**, should be read for a very fully documented account of all the economic, political, and managerial, as well as technological factors which contribute to a disaster. Much earlier, but in a somewhat similar vein though in an English context in the early 1930s, is part of Nevil Shute's autobiography, *Slide Rule* 1968, Pan, relating to the airships R100 and R101.

74

A direct head-on impact calculation

Stevenson (7) has given interesting curves for the remaining undamaged length as calculated for a 45 m (150 ft) long jet transport (a DC-8), crashing normally at its front for various speeds, into a rigid surface. His results are derived from writing the equation of motion as

$$v\frac{dv}{dx} = \frac{F}{k(l-x) + M_c},$$ (1)

where v is the speed of the moving aircraft mass at time t after impact and x is the crushed length (Fig. 41); k is the mass per unit length of fuselage

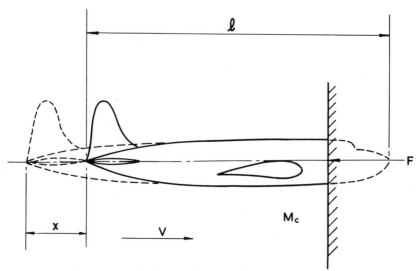

Fig. 41. Model of aircraft impinging against a rigid surface

and l its initial length. M_c is the concentrated mass at the wings (fuel and engines, etc.) and F denotes the crushing strength of the aircraft. Equation (1) after integration leads to

$$\left(\frac{v}{v_0}\right)^2 = 1 - \frac{2F}{kv_0^2}\ln\left(1 - \frac{x}{L}\right),$$ (2)

where v_0 is the original aircraft speed and $L = l + (M_c/k)$. Any earth scooping or ploughing is neglected (see p. 87). The aircraft mass is said

75

to be reasonably approximated by considering it to be uniformly distributed along its length (at 1500 kg/m or 1000 lb/ft) with a concentrated mass of 68 100 kg (150 000 lb) at mid-length for the wings and engine, etc. Once the wings reach the rigid surface, the latter mass is abruptly removed from the calculations so that the retardation rate suddenly increases from about 1 g to 3·4 g as Fig. 43 shows. The remaining crushed length for various initial impact speeds for the jet transport example considered is shown in Fig. 42. The total crash time for this DC-8 model, impinging at

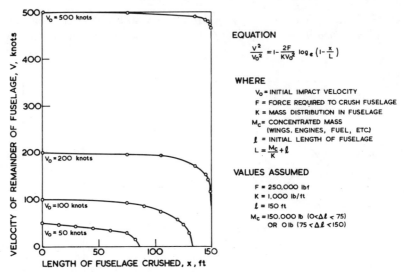

EQUATION

$$\frac{V^2}{V_0^2} = 1 - \frac{2F}{KV_0^2} \log_e \left(1 - \frac{x}{L}\right)$$

WHERE

V_0 = INITIAL IMPACT VELOCITY
F = FORCE REQUIRED TO CRUSH FUSELAGE
K = MASS DISTRIBUTION IN FUSELAGE
M_c = CONCENTRATED MASS
    (WINGS, ENGINES, FUEL, ETC)
l = INITIAL LENGTH OF FUSELAGE
$L = \frac{M_c}{K} + l$

VALUES ASSUMED

F = 250,000 lbf
K = 1,000 lb/ft
l = 150 ft
M_c = 150,000 lb (0<Δl < 75)
    OR 0 lb (75 < Δl <150)

Fig. 42. Crushed length of fuselage after impinging against a rigid vertical surface

108 knots so that 4 m (13 ft) of fuselage would remain, is 1·04 s. A container mounted aft in the fuselage and which could only tolerate a loading of say 3·4 g would, by reference to Fig. 43, break-away when 22·5 m (75 ft) of fuselage had been crushed, to become a missile.

This model is, of course, greatly oversimplified and even the gross mechanics is wanting; the impact process is probably more realistically compared with that of the mushrooming of an impacting bullet, see p. 229 of ref. (5), i.e., with extensive mass accretion in the impact zone.

Full scale aircraft impact testing (7, 8)

Some few detailed studies of aircraft in process of impact, or after impact, have been or are now being made and it is worthwhile to note some of

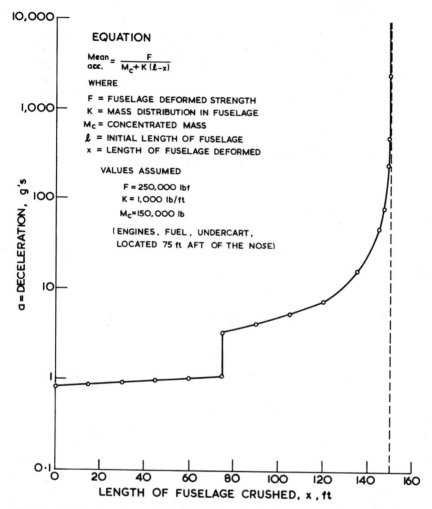

Fig. 43. Calculated mean retardation of fuselage while deforming against a rigid surface

them. Impressive, and the most recent, is that now being conducted at The Langley Research Center, USA, where a lunar landing research facility has been converted to one for investigating structural crash effects in general aviation type aircraft. A full scale plane of length 14 m and weight 2720 kg, suspended by two swing cables (drawn back to a predetermined height and then released to perform a pendulum swing from a gantry 73 m high (Fig. 44)), is allowed to crash into an horizontal surface of reinforced concrete. Aeroplane attitude, yaw, roll and attack angle, and velocity can all be preselected. Data acquired on board is brought out through an umbilical cable; on-board accelerometers, load cells, extensometers, and strain gauges are used. At impact, the free body speeds in the seven aircraft tests conducted, up to July 1975, lay between 13 and 27 m/s

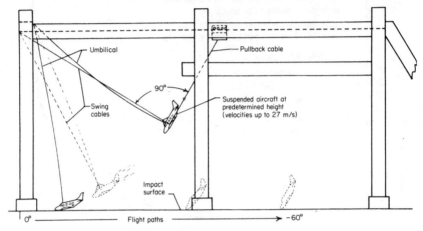

Fig. 44. Full-scale aircraft crash-test technique

(Fig. 45), and took place against a background grid 1 m square, being photographed at speeds in the range 20–2000 frames per second.

Figure 46 shows a sequence of photographs for crash test No. 6 of Fig. 45 at 1/20 s intervals during a typical crash at a speed of 27 m/s (or ∼ 46 miles/h); an upward retardation of 660 g was measured on the structure at the point of impact for 2 ms and a retardation of 275 g for 5 ms resulted from a least squares fit to the raw data; oscillations lasted for 0·11 s.

Indications of how scale testing and modelling laws may be applied to structural testing is given by Holmes and Colton (9), which contains an example of how damage caused by impulsive loads on scaled-down aircraft fuselages may be applied to full scale work.

In a paper by Wittlin and Gammon (21), pp. 63–82, predictions of the gross deformation, configuration, and deflections of structural elements with time after impact, from using a digital computer program to model an aeroplane impact, are compared with the results of a crash test into a

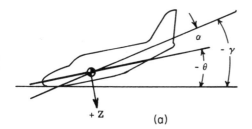

γ   Flight-path angle
α   Angle of attack
θ   Pitch angle,
      θ = γ + α

(a)

Crash test 2,

Crash test 4,

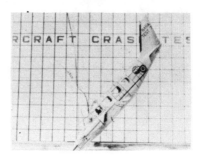

Crash test 6,

Crash test 7,

(b)

Fig. 45. (a) *Aircraft crash-test;* (b) *Photographs showing aircraft crash attitudes for four crash-tests*

Test No.	Pitch angle θ°	Vertical speed (in/s)	Horizontal speed (in/s)
2	−12·00	7·35	25·68
4	4·25	6·97	26·47
6	14·00	7·63	25·76
7	−47·25	21·09	19·32

45° dirt barrier at 13·7 m/s (45 ft/s) on a full scale helicopter. The mathematical model of the aeroplane is indicated in Fig. 47(a), and in Fig. 47(b), the post-test deflected position of the engine and cabin structure. In Fig. 47(c), the actual aircraft is shown and in Fig. 47(d), the helicopter after impact.

(a) Primary impact.

(b) 0.05 s after contact.

(c) 0.10 s after contact.

(d) 0.15 s after contact.

(e) 0.20 s after contact.

(f) 0.25 s after contact.

| (g) 0.30 s after contact. | (h) 0.35 s after contact. |

(i) 0.40 s after contact.

Fig. 46. Sequence of photographs for crash-test 6; $\gamma = -16\cdot5°$, $\theta = 14\cdot0°$, $\alpha = 30\cdot5°$

Foam beds for aircraft overrun arrest

When landing in distress, a significant factor with heavy aircraft† is forward speed, and it has long been recognized that what is wanted is 'aircraft that land slowly and don't burn-up'. The clean separation of landing gear and engine mountings without any rupture of fuel tank walls is required but difficult to attain. At best, a fuselage belly should be able to accept any predicted sliding load condition with plastic collapse (due to aircraft weight and sliding friction), be a relatively slow process, and progressively absorb kinetic energy. Experimental results and the considerations which apply for arresting civil aircraft which overrun are presented in refs (15–18).

Trials into gravel beds 305 mm (12 in) deep, of sieve sizes 19 mm ($\frac{3}{4}$ in)

† The Turkish DC-10 aeroplane which crashed outside Paris in March 1974 causing the death of over 330 people, was said to be made by a low level impact at 800 km/h (500 miles/h) and to have created a forest scar of over 450 m length and 90 m wide (22).

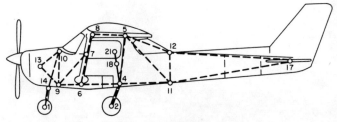

<u>Not shown</u>
Left wing masses: 15, 19
Left wing and strut members: 8–15, 15–19, 6–19
Right wing masses: 16, 20
Right wing and strut members: 8–16, 16–20, 6–16

(a)

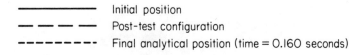

———————— Initial position
— — — — — Post-test configuration
- - - - - - - - Final analytical position (time = 0.160 seconds)

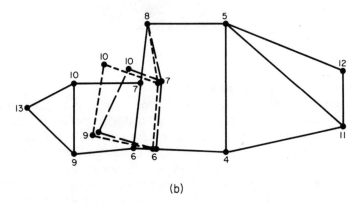

(b)

Note: (1) Diagonal element 7.9 Omitted for clarity
      (2) Mass 13 not shown in deflected positions
          for clarity

Fig. 47. (a) *Twenty-one-mass, 32-member mathematical model for aeroplane;*
         (b) *Comparison of test and analytical aeroplane deformations;*
         (c) *Side view of aeroplane prior to crash-test;*
         (d) *Side view of aeroplane after crash-test*

82

(c)

(d)

and 38 mm ($1\frac{1}{2}$ in) and density $1\cdot4$ kg/cm³ (88 lb/ft³), were initially conducted (Fig. 48). Among other results the smaller gravel was found to give the higher retardation rate, f. Gravel spray pattern† was recognized as being important for anticipating the damage to airframes and engines.

Fig. 48. Canberra *wheel tracks showing directional stability*

A *Lightning P1B* aircraft, all-up weight 11 800 kg (26 000 lb), was tested on a bed $8\cdot2$–$12\cdot2$ m (27–40 ft) wide and length 122 m (400 ft) with 19 mm ($\frac{3}{4}$ in) gravel, using tyres 84×17 cm (33 in $\times$ 6·75 in) and inflation pressure 1793 kN/m² (260 lbf/in²). Towing the aircraft through the gravel gave a wheel drag coefficient of 0·41. (In dynamic tests pitching was avoided because of a tapered entry or by gradually increasing the depth of gravel over $18\cdot3$ to 61 m (60 to 200 ft).) Free-running and braked entries at up to $33\cdot5$ m/s (110 ft/s) provided mean values of f of $\sim 0\cdot58$ g with $f_{max} \simeq 1$ g; f – retardation/distance curves are shown in Fig. 49(a). Good directional stability is achieved in all these arrester beds. Penetration was about 229 mm (9 in); when the bed depth was increased to 458 mm (18 in), f was increased to between 0·7 and 1 g. Tests with a *Canberra*, weight $\sim$ 13 600 kg (30 000 lb), gave lower magnitudes of f at 0·4 g to 0·8 g; f maximum was again $\sim$ 1 g but see Fig. 49(b).

† Refer to p. 71 and ref. (**11**) in Part II.

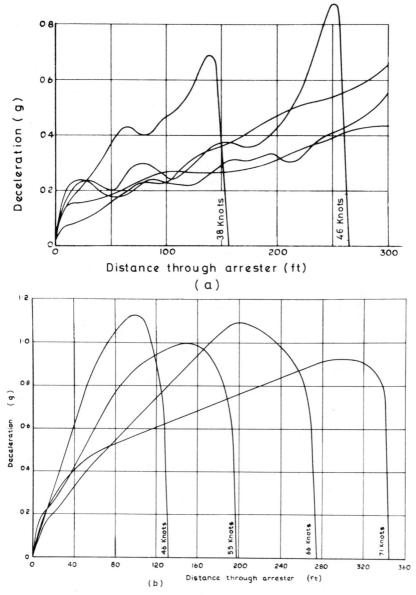

Fig. 49. Typical deceleration–distance curves
(a) Lightning, (b) Canberra

85

Generally it is thought that $f = 0.7\ g$ to $1\ g$ should be aimed for in arrester beds both for passenger comfort, with a lap-strap safety belt in a forward facing seat, and to preserve the main undercarriage legs.

Water as an arrester medium is unsuitable because it requires high installation costs (excavation) and maintenance (dirt, leaves, freezing-over, evaporation, and bird attraction with strike hazards). Sand and soils are unsuitable because wheel drag variation would be large, due to changing water content. Coarse gravel does not have these drawbacks.

An aircraft arriving at ~ 61 m/s (200 ft/s) would require an arrester length of 274 m (900 ft) if $f = 0.7$ g.

Planing, i.e., tyre lift, is developed through the gravel at higher speeds, and when the speed is sufficiently high it may equal the vertical downward force. Increase in gravel depth increases the mean retardation but not in direct proportion (16). In ref. (17) a report is made of the arresting trials of a 1/9·3 scale model VC-10, model weight 148 kg (327 lb) and VC-10 weight 163 500 kg (360 000 lb). The model was fired into beds of gravel and sintered fuel ash pellets of various depths from an air operated catapult with take-off and landing unbraked wheel speeds of 45·7 m/s (150 ft/s). The results indicated that a VC-10 at take-off could be stopped, with good directional stability, in 152 m (500 ft) from a speed of 41 m/s (134 ft/s) using 61 cm (24 in) depth of either material.

The previously described tests dealt with small aircraft with single-wheel undercarriage units but in ref. (17) the investigations described were extended to large aircraft with multi-wheel bogie undercarriages. Arresting tests as described in the report by Gwynne (18) were performed with a *Comet 3B* at a greatest landing weight (fully fuelled) of 54 400 kg and speeds of up to ~ 29 m/s (94 ft/s) in test beds of urea formaldehyde. It was found that the retardation was independent of entry speed – at about $0.5\ g$ – and that significant drag was contributed by the leading and trailing wheels of a bogie arrangement. At the conclusion of testing it was considered that the design of foam arresters was possible for airfields where overrun hazards exist, undercarriage units not being seriously overstressed due to foam drag loads.

The maximum crushable depth of the foam layers was 80 per cent of the original depth; for more than this it becomes a consolidated layer. At speeds of 20 m/s (66 ft/s), the *Comet 3B* was arrested in 55 m in a time of about 4 s.

Foam layer density controls the wheel penetration depth; foam does not support combustion and aviation fuel spill is rapidly absorbed with fire

86

confined to the surface. In February 1968 it was estimated that gravel arrester beds could be installed for £10 000 per 100 ft width of runway.

Damage to property

It is evident (1) that the Royal Aircraft Establishment, Farnborough, England have considerable knowledge of the extent and intensity of damage inflicted on property due to aircraft wreckage. Recently, however, damage from aircraft unintentionally or (potentially) intentionally attacking property, e.g., from hijacked planes, has assumed special importance in connection with the protection of nuclear power plant† and, to a lesser extent, off-shore oil rigs, communication towers, and the like.

Airframe crashworthiness (9)

Crashworthiness refers to the capability of an airframe structure to maintain a protective shell‡ around occupants during a crash, and ability to subject any human occupant to a retardation rate which can be tolerated. The topic is treated at some length in ref. (10) which contains much useful information, though mainly for application to light aircraft.§ The design of crashworthy envelopes must necessarily be coupled with knowledge of the loads which human occupants – large retardation or acceleration rates – can withstand.

Conspicuous factors in achieving these are:

1. The design of a structure which, on making contact with the earth, reduces the gouging and scooping of soil and hence reduces retardation rates and associated forces,
2. Ensuring that any external component breakaway is safe, and
3. Reinforcing cockpit and cabin structures to withstand large forces with little, or without any, plastic deformation.

The scooping-up and ploughing of earth by a collapsed fuselage (Fig. 50), contributes to increased rate of retardation because (a) a mass of earth must be quickly accelerated in the scooping operation, i.e., there is momentum exchange, and (b), the ploughing results in an increased force

† Any tendency to depressurization because of penetration of an aircraft cabin by a bullet from the gun of a hijacker will usually be well countered by the aircraft air-booster pumps; their supply rate would be much greater than the leak rate. See also the refs of ref. (20).
‡ Significant detail about bird strikes against the view or windscreen of the cockpit, and bird ingestion by engines so that disintegrating blades become missiles or shrapnel, and penetrate the aircraft cabin, does not seem to be readily available.
§ See also papers in ref. (21).

87

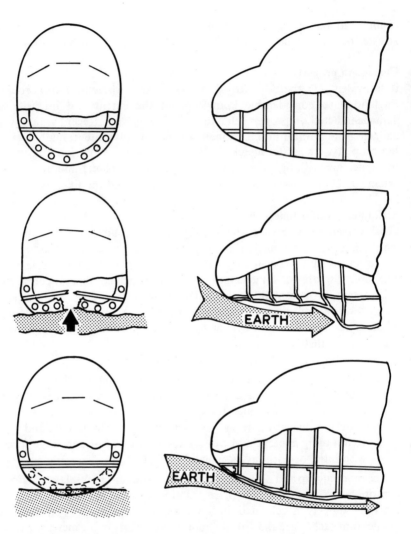

Fig. 50. Method of reinforcing nose structure to provide increased resistance to vertical loads and to reduce earth scooping

being continuously applied during the whole retardation process. The severity of the primary impact process very much depends on the distance available for dissipating any initial kinetic energy. For aircraft impinging against the earth with a velocity vector substantially parallel to it, there is usually a relatively long distance available for arrest in scooping and ploughing (arrester beds neglected), but where the velocity vector makes a large angle with an earth surface, arrest must obviously be relatively rapid with retardations and forces generally much higher than in the more-or-less horizontal case (when other things are the same), see p. 75. Comparable empirical survivability curves for these two directions of arrest are given in Fig. 51. Longitudinal crashworthiness is enhanced by designing

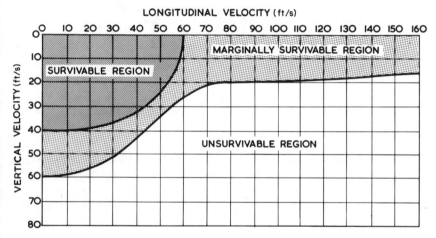

Fig. 51. *Initial impact velocities based on accident case histories of military and civilian aircraft*

to reduce scooping and ploughing at the fuselage front and belly, where they will be encountered, so that a surface skidding process is best aimed for. One such design from ref. (9) is shown in Fig. 50. Besides considering cabin floor structure strength,† some compressive buckling failure of a fuselage requires to be envisaged, due to the large angular acceleration rates (whip) induced by the impulse at impact tending to change attitude pitch to align the 'plane with the surface.

Vertical impacts would seem to be minimized by providing seats which have a relatively long vertical energy-absorbing stroke and/or including a

† The sudden blowing-out of a poorly designed, and poorly secured aft bulk cargo door, due to an internal pressure excess of about 28 kN/m² (4 lbf/in²), led to the collapse of part of the cabin floor of the DC-10 and the destruction of all of its flight control capability (22).

sub-cabin floor crushable region of depth sufficient to adequately absorb the vertical energy of impact.†

Crashworthiness as it touches on wings, empennage, landing gear, engine mounts, and the necessity for strong structural framing around emergency exits, are also discussed in ref. (10).

OCCUPANT PROTECTION

General remarks

There are four specific aspects to aircraft crashworthiness as it pertains to occupants involved in an aircraft collision process. These are:

1. The occupant acceleration environment: this pertains to the intensity and duration, and hence tolerance, of the retardations experienced by occupants (with belt 'tie-down' assumed intact) during a crash.
2. Occupant environment hazards: barriers, projections, and loose or broken-away equipment in the immediate vicinity of the occupant may cause contact injuries.
3. Tie-down chain strength: this concerns the strength of any linkage or device which will prevent an occupant, cargo, or equipment from becoming a missile during a crash sequence.
4. Postcrash hazards: great threats to occupant survival are posed by fire, drowning or exposure, etc., following the impact sequence.

Two phases have often been identified for a crash: the *dynamic* one during which the accident or an impact occurs and develops, and the *static* phase during which survivors evacuate the vehicle, to which aspect 4 above applies.

Whilst category 4 is outside our close concern, it must be said that crash fuel fires, smoke, and the gaseous toxicity of furnishings and other aircraft materials, probably present a greater hazard to life than any of the other three.

The above aspects of a crash were early identified in a more general way by De Haven (11) in 1952‡ and are worthy of note since they have wide applicability.

† Ezra and Fay in *Dynamic Response of Structures* (23), p. 341, suggest that since structures high in the fuselage undergo lower acceleration in a crash than those below due to energy absorption by the structure itself, seats might be better if suspended from the upper fuselage structure. This would also remove passengers from difficulties due to floor buckling.

‡ See the reference to De Haven in R. Nader's book (19), p. 69.

With passengers in an aircraft cabin or automobile in mind, De Haven observed that there are four very useful and simple basic packaging principles which should be kept in mind when designing for safety; these are:

(a) The 'shipping container' should not open up and spill its contents, or collapse on its contents under reasonable or expected conditions of impact.
(b) Articles contained in the packages should be held and immobilized inside the container, to prevent movement and resultant damage against the inside of the package itself.
(c) The means of immobilizing the contents inside the container must transmit forces to the strongest part of the contained articles.
(d) The inside of the container must be designed to cushion and distribute impact forces over maximum surface area of the contents, and have 'yield qualities' to increase deceleration time in case they break loose from their restraints.

Many outstanding students of aircraft safety design have long espoused these principles.

The first of De Haven's principles for cabin integrity is reckoned to be met by general aviation aircraft as long as the impact is not so severe as to give rise to a retardation of 6–7 g; the fourth principle is said to be ignored by aircraft designers so that 4·5 m/s (15 ft/s) impact speeds cause injuries (**12**).

Body behaviour and tolerances: Seats, seat belts, and the physical environment mainly in relation to light aircraft

In the course of sudden retardations, unrestrained or partially restrained (by a seat belt) occupants are likely to flail about in a disintegrating cabin. and various parts of the body may strike (or be struck by) objects which penetrate or crush it; see, for example, the diagrammatic representation in Fig. 52. Note also that about 80 per cent of deaths in transportation vehicle crashes are a result of head impact,† and further, that the serious injury rate for automotive transport is 1000 per cent greater than the death rate but only 50 per cent greater for general aviation.

Strike envelopes for restrained occupants vary according to the form of seat belt restraint (lap or lap-and-shoulder harness, etc.), and seat orientation, and are discussed in detail in ref. (**12**) and in papers in ref. (**9**).

† 55 000 deaths per year in the USA are due to automobile accidents and about 1200 to aviation.

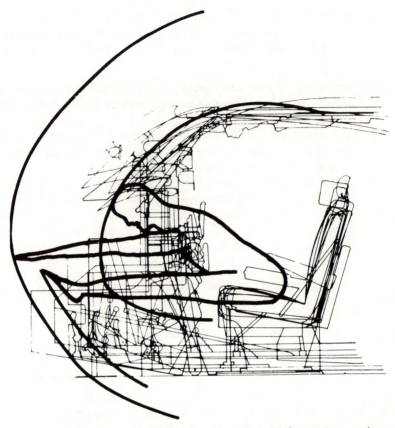

Fig. 52. Area of forward flailing (95th percentile) with seat belt restraint, superimposed on scale drawings of 11 general aviation aircraft. (After Swearingham (12).)

Envelopes are defined by the movement of totally unsecured parts of the body – extended limbs, head and torso flexure – with some added allowance for a torso movement from a seat of about 100 mm (Fig. 53); the strike envelope is believed to be changed when the occupant is subjected to a 4 g acceleration.

Head impact against a flat surface is so injurious as to have necessitated particular investigation and some relevant tolerance data are discussed on p. 49; this results in the Gadd Severity Index criterion.† It is stated that impact into a rigid surface by a human head at 6 m/s (20 ft/s) cannot be

† See p. 53.

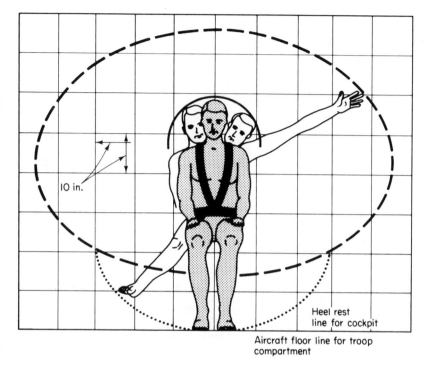

10 in.

Heel rest
line for cockpit

Aircraft floor line for troop
compartment

Fig. 53. Full-restraint extremity strike envelope (front view)

withstood without interposing an appreciable thickness of energy absorbing and load-spreading material; Fig. 54 compares the retardation-time
pulses for tests of head impact at 4·6 m/s (15 ft/s) and 9·2 m/s (30 ft/s)
against a common rigid instrument panel (case No. 2) and against a
yielding half-cylinder of aluminium (case No. 1) (12). The enormous
reduction in retardation magnitude, and the increased time of arrest is
clearly evident, and hence the latter is conducive to injury reduction.
Curves showing the results of designing for protection of the head on
impact by using polyethylene, polystyrene bead board and semi-rigid
urethane, are given in ref. (10). Padding for protection against head
impact is equally applicable for protection of other parts of the body.

The principles and mechanics of belt restraint, using lap and shoulder
harness systems, are indicated in Fig. 55; included are inertia reels,
materials, and connections and anchorages are again discussed at length in
ref. (10); seat pitching is also important. (In ref. (6) it is stated. that

93

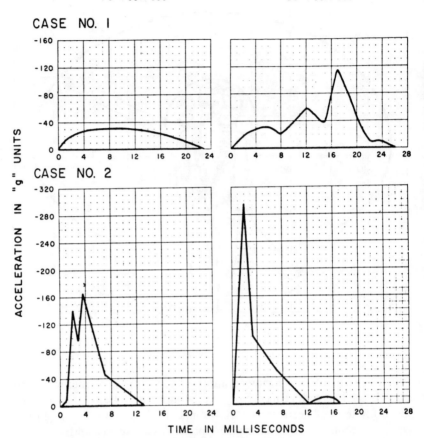

15 Feet/sec   30 Feet/sec

CASE NO. 1

CASE NO. 2

ACCELERATION IN "g" UNITS

TIME IN MILLISECONDS

Fig. 54. A comparison of the head retardation–time pulses for striking against a hard instrument panel and a yielding half-cylinder of aluminium

passengers restrained only by a seat belt, took a violent forward displacement of the upper torso which brought their head into contact with the seat in front, their chest coming into contact with their thighs and knees. Back facing seats would obviate this kind of injury.)

With many single shoulder-strap seat belt combinations, tolerance is estimated to be 17 g, but is probably nearer to 30 g. The upper limit for forward impact, with double shoulder harness and seat belt, is said to be about 40 g (Fig. 55).

94

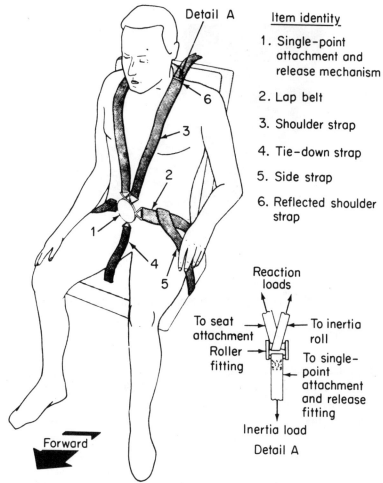

Detail A

Item identity

1. Single-point attachment and release mechanism

2. Lap belt

3. Shoulder strap

4. Tie-down strap

5. Side strap

6. Reflected shoulder strap

Reaction loads

To seat attachment

To inertia roll

Roller fitting

To single-point attachment and release fitting

Inertia load

Detail A

Forward

Fig. 55. Forward-facing harness concept (improved lateral restraint)

Preferably, lap belts in aircraft should cross the iliac crest and be taken back at 45° to the floor, not just across the thighs and to the floor; then not only the pelvic region is restrained (Fig. 56). If the advantages of various seat facing directions are examined then the aft-facing seat, with a head rest, is notable for giving stability and support to a potentially flailing body (i.e., as compared with a forward-facing seat), in an arresting situation.

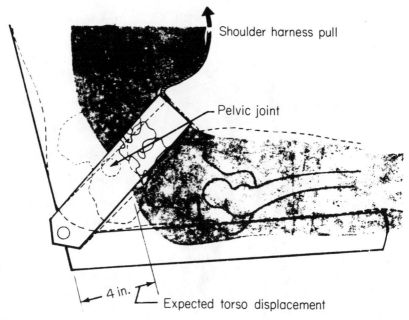

Shoulder harness pull

Pelvic joint

4 in.

Expected torso displacement

Fig. 56. Pelvis rotation and 'submarining' caused by high longitudinal forces combined with moderate vertical forces

On p. 41, aspects of airbag usage in motor car crash situations were discussed, but in a recent article, Snyder (31) p. 59, has evaluated at length inflatable airbags for restraining aircraft passengers. It is imagined for a jet transport, that a bag about one half the size of its automotive counterpart only, would be permissible. Bags would be deployed from a position in front of the occupant's knees to cushion both knees and torso and from the seat back in front of the occupant; they would be supplemented by an energy absorbing structure. Fabric, rather than film bags would be preferred, to give a high strength-to-weight ratio, to mitigate temperature effects due to storage and deployment, and to be highly resistant to snag or tear. Crash sensor types are (a) predictive, (b) impact or (c) combination. Automotive crash conditions are different from those of aircraft (the crash pulse is different), and despite many common features, Snyder's conclusion is that, at the moment, the NASA 'Ames' air transport rearward-facing seat, or one of the inflatable webbing restraints, would offer best all-round crash protection to aircraft occupants. A significant consideration for

96

aircraft would be the weight penalty of about 3·63 kg (8 lb) per occupant, i.e., about 1½ tons for a wide-bodied transport.

Vertebral injury (and brain concussion) has been studied for more than thirty years because of ejection injuries from a seated position sustained by fighter pilots during emergency egress (22). Rapid ejection increases spinal curvature and causes excessive bending (in pulse rise times of 5 to 14 ms), which with large axial compression gives rise to anterior lip and compressive fracture of the thoracic vertebrae (Fig. 57), and see refs (9, 12).

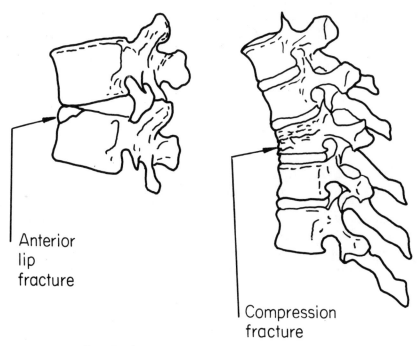

Anterior
lip
fracture

Compression
fracture

Fig. 57. Showing anterior lip and compression fracture

Typical triangular body acceleration design pulses (Fig. 58), corresponding to the 95th percentile, vary according to whether the ejection direction is longitudinal, vertical or lateral. They also slightly differ as between cabin and cockpit, and Rotary and Light Fixed Wing Aircraft, and Fixed Wing Transport Aircraft. Typically (as assessed from surviving accident cases), peak g-tolerances lie between 16 (lateral) and 48 (vertical), with average g-levels between 8 and 24 for pulse durations of 0·060 to 0·200 s.

97

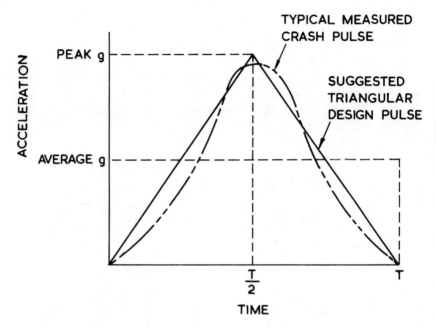

Fig. 58. Typical impact pulse for all aircraft types

Well worth perusing is Swearingham's *Aviation Structures Responsible for Trauma in Crash Decelerations* (**12**). A notable example of the case for protection against vertical impact† is that of 6 men found in a sitting position, with seat belts still fastened who, in effect, fell vertically through 30 m (100 ft) in a suddenly arrested aircraft; they were all killed. The retardation rate was evidently far too great; apparently there was only 100 mm available for crushing through the seats, and 100 mm through the fuselage; an aircraft deceleration rate of about 100 *g* was probably imposed during impact. Massive internal injuries were sustained by all the men who, when found, appeared to be sleeping. Evidently seats should not be of a frail design that allows them to crush easily, so dissipating little speed and permitting bottoming-out against a rigid structure with high *g*-forces.

Selected and well-regarded by Swearingham (**12**) is the Beech Aircraft Corporation, who as early as 1953, put into the (light) *Bonanza* plane, a long nose, wing crash absorption, reinforced channel sections surrounding the cabin-capsule, a heavy keel forward of the panel, an instrument panel

† See also the circumstances of the Markham Main Colliery Disaster, p. 121, Part V.

mounted on shearable shock mounts, a strong seat tie-down to the basic structure, and installation of shoulder harness (Fig. 59); experience showed that these items paid-off well in terms of protection.

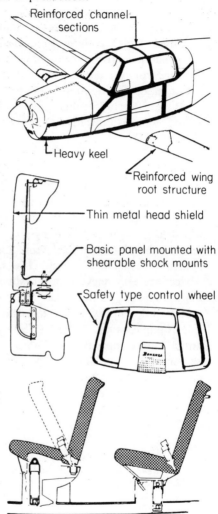

A. Tho BEECHCRAFT Bonanza's long nose section provides gradual impact deceleration.

B. The BEECHCRAFT Bonanza's wing design provides crash shock absorption in addition to its rugged design which has been tested to over 8.4 G's which is 47 percent above government required safety margins.

C. The Bonanza's fuselage has reinforced keel section providing occupant protection against crashes and lessening crash damage.

D. The Bonanza's reinforced cockpit provides a strong crash-resistant passenger compartment or structurally - reinforced capsule for maximum occupant protection.

E. The Bonanza instrument panel is installed with shearable shock mounts on basic instrument panel with a thin gauge soft metal head shield to lessen the possibilities of passenger injuries in event of crash landing.

F. The new Bonanza is equipped with body supporting safety-type control wheel to reduce chest and lung injuries in event of crash landing.

G. The Bonanza seats and safety belts are securely mounted to the basic spar truss with the front seat backs hinged to swing forward out of head range of occupants in the rear seat to provide a maximum of passenger protection.

Fig. 59. 'Crash Safety Can Be Engineered' from ref. (**12**). *Special features – Beech Aircraft Corporation*

99

Specifically for light aircraft (but many of these features apply for other vehicular types), cockpit regions should provide good structural crash integrity, bearing in mind the possibility of overturning. Instrument panels, within flailing distance and especially for the head, sharp edges or protruding bodies should be removed and crushable material applied. Pedals in tunnels which collapse onto the legs (causing injury and preventing escape), and control wheels and columns should be designed to yield under pressure from the chest, and not become penetrating weapons.

Commanding attention is the volume of 35 papers on Aircraft Crashworthiness (9) (1975); this explores in depth many of the subjects referred to above and is indicative of contemporary US research in this field; see also ref. (21).

Cargo restraint

Cargo restraining devices are chosen with cargo volume in mind; small items when not carried by occupants or stored in boxes, containers or nets, will probably be restrained with nuts attached to aircraft floor fittings, whilst large items are held by chains, ropes and cables, etc. Acceptable floor loading levels and tolerable load movements for designing restraint systems are detailed in ref. (14). Energy absorbing and load limiting devices are very relevant to this situation (5, 20).

Recalling the frontal crash analysis, see Figs. 42 and 43, it will be appreciated that heavy, bulky items should not be carried behind passengers. For example, in ref. (21), p. 64 it is noted that in designing an agricultural aircraft, the hopper is placed ahead of the pilot; it is conceived to act also as crushable material on impact. By designing the cockpit as a protective cage with seat and harness of compatible strength, the chances of a pilot's survival in a crash are greatly improved.

REFERENCES

(1) WALKER, P. B., 'The Scientific Investigation of Aircraft Accidents', James Clayton Lecture L3/65, *Proc. Inst. Mech. Engrs.*, 1964–5, **179**, Pt. 1.
(2) BARLAY, S., *Aircrash Detective* 1975 (Coronet Books, Hodder and Stoughton, London).
(3) BEATY, D., *The Human Factor in Aircraft Accidents* 1969 (Scientific Book Club).
(4) ICAD. Aircraft Accident Digests.
(5) JOHNSON, W., *Impact Strength of Materials* 1972, p. 306 (Arnold, London).
(6) *The Ditching of a DC-9 Aircraft, Friday, 2 May 1970 in the Caribbean Sea*, Nat. Trans. Safety Board, Report No. ASS-72-2.

(7) STEVENSON, H. T., *Ten Years of Crash Recovery Research* 1965. (NRCC, NAE MISC 38).

(8) VAUGHAN, V. L., Jr., and ALFARA-BON, E., *Impact Dynamics Research Facility for Full Scale Aircraft Crash Testing* 1976 (NASA, TN D-8179).

(9) Eds. SACZALSKI, K. J., *et al.*, *Aircraft Crashworthiness* 1975 (Univ. Press of Virginia, Charlottesville).

(10) *Crash Survival Design Guide AD 733 358*, Revised Oct. 1971 (Eustis Directorate, U.S. Army Air Mobility Research and Development Laboratory).

(11) DE HAVEN, H., *Accidental Survival, Airplane and Automobile Passengers* 1952 (Cornell Univ. Med. Coll.).

(12) SWEARINGHAM, J. J. *General Aviation Structures Directly Responsible for Trauma in Crash Decelerations* 1971 (Dept. of Transportation, Federal Aviation Administration, Office of Aviation Medicine, Washington D.C.).

(13) ORNE, D., and LIU, Y. K., 'A Mathematical Model of Spinal Response to Impact', *J. Biomechanics* 1971, **4**, 49.

(14) HUNDAL, M. S., McLAY, R. W., and FOLSOM, L., 'Design and Analysis of an Energy Absorbing Restraint System for Light Aircraft Crash Impact', *Trans. ASME, J. Eng. Ind.* 1974, **96B**, 495.

(15) BADE, E., *Soft Ground Arresting of Civil Aircraft* 1968, RAE. Tech. Report 68032.

(16) BADE, E., *Soft Ground Arresting of Civil Aircraft – Influence of Gravel Depth and Tyre Inflation Pressure* 1969, RAE. Tech. Report, 69001.

(17) BADE, E., and MINTER, E. M., *Soft Ground Arresting of Civil Aircraft – Scaled Model VC-10 Tests in Gravel and Sintered Fuel Ash Pellets* 1971, RAE. Tech. Report, 71015.

(18) GWYNNE, G. M., *Urea Formaldehyde Foamed Plastic Emergency Arresters for Civil Aircraft* 1974, RAE. Tech. Report, 74002.

(19) NADER, R., *Unsafe at Any Speed* 1973, Bantam, London.

(20) JOHNSON, W., and REID, S. R., 'Metallic Energy Dissipating Systems' 1978, Review to be published in *Applied Mechanics Reviews*.

(21) Eds. SACZALSKI, K. J., and PILKEY, W. D., *Measurement and Prediction of Structural and Biodynamic Crash-Impact Response* 1976, ASME Conference.

(22) EDDY, P., POTTER, E., and PAGE, B., *Destination Disaster* 1976 (Hart-Davies, MacGibbon Ltd).

(23) EZRA, A. A., and FAY, R. J., *Dynamic Response of Structures*, Eds HERRMANN, G., and PERRONE, N., 1972 (Pergamon Press, Oxford).

101

Part IV: Ship collisions†

Ship accidents and collisions always attract great attention because of the sheer massiveness of the colliding bodies involved and because it is an event we rarely have the opportunity of actually witnessing. The cost of repair or recovery has always been enormous but today's collisions take on another dimension of importance, in that its scale – actual or potential – has great consequences for the environment‡. Even gigantic damage or losses such as that of the *Titanic*§ seem in the past never to have stimulated considerations of (passive) design against impact and such design as there has been appears to have been confined to warships. A comprehensive history of warship design against forms of impact is not to be found though perhaps the beginning of studies for protecting metal ships is the interesting entry associated with Bertram Hopkinson‖ in the *Encyclopaedia Brittanica*¶: 'An internal bulkhead 2 in in thickness was fitted as a protection against torpedo explosion††; "Blisters" are being fitted to increase this protection still further . . .' A more modern note was struck (literally) in the Cod War of 1975 when frigate repairs of about £1 million were disclosed and protection to hulls of $\frac{3}{8}$ in thickness was supposedly to be given by securing rubber fenders to the plating, railway sleepers and sandbags also being attached using inch-thick frames.

It has been suggested that prestressed concrete may replace steel as a construction material for some large ships (because construction and run-

---

† For a survey of the slamming impact of the forward bottom of ships in a seaway, ship-bow flare impact or the hydrodynamic loading and structural response of surface ships, see the *Proc. of the Sixth Int. Ship Structures Congress*, Vol. I, Committee Report II 3. Liquid cargo sloshing effects are also discussed.

‡ An unusual occurrence which violently affected the environment took place in December 1917 when a French munitioner carrying nearly half a million pounds of TNT collided with an empty Belgian relief ship in the harbour of Halifax, Nova Scotia, Canada. The resulting explosion, perhaps the largest artificial explosion in history up to that date, caused the death of over 2000 and injury of 6000 inhabitants and destroyed the town almost completely over 300 acres.

§ This disaster occurred 12 April 1912 when the liner moving at 21 knots, 'cut smoothly a 300 ft gash in her double bottom' on colliding with an iceberg. She sank in 3 hours and 1494 persons were drowned.

‖ 1874–1918, Professor of Engineering, University of Cambridge.

¶ Vol. 3, p. 222, 1946 Edition.

†† Underwater explosions, with some studies of plastic deformation, were greatly researched during World Wars I and II and are reported in ref. (1). These include, among other things, the determination of pressure intensity for a given charge weight at a given distance, scaling laws, and detonation or gas bubble movement and oscillation beneath the water surface.

ning costs are reduced) in the course of the next decade; high strength and light weight, with fibre bonding, offer new prospects. Should large ships of such materials be built, associated brittle impact damage will need to be conspicuously considered.

There is not much information about ship protection against collision and most of the little there is, is outlined below.

Minorsky's analysis (2)

The penetration of one ship by another during collision has assumed great importance with the use of nuclear power plant for propulsive purposes.†

Fig. 60. '*The bows of a Soviet freighter embedded in the passenger ferry* Queen of Victoria *30 miles west of Vancouver. A mother, her baby son, and a teenage girl were killed by the 15 000-ton freighter. The ship penetrated almost to the centre of the ferry, which was carrying 540 passengers and crew and 150 vehicles.*' (The Guardian, *4 August 1970*)

† According to the *Guardian*, 3 February 1977, there are about 270 nuclear-powered submarines and surface warships in service with the Soviet and NATO navies, and three nuclear merchant ships in the West: the American *Savannah*, the Japanese *Matsu*, and the German *Otto Hahn*.

It has become essential to endeavour to estimate the structural strength of a hull of a nuclear ship, outboard of any reactor plant, so that it may safely protect the latter in the event of a collision.

Detailed analytical calculations are not feasible for ship structures where there is progressive plastic failure by panel buckling, shearing, tearing, crushing, bending, and twisting of plates, etc., as the typical extensive complex plastic deformation of damaged ships shows (Figs. 60–62). (See also Fig. 69 and refs (3) and (11).)

Fig. 61. The bow of the Florida *in collision with the White Star liner* Baltic *c. 1910 (photograph provided by Dr. N. Jones (6))*

Fig. 62. A 9 970-ton Chilean cargo vessel, the Maipo, *snapped its mooring ropes as it was preparing to leave Birkenhead and rammed a 15 376-ton British iron ore carrier,* The Knightsgarth. *The* Maipo *sliced into* The Knightsgarth *amidships and ended up embedded 10 ft deep in its side. Members of both crews were shaken by the impact; no one was hurt.'* (The Guardian, *3 November 1973*)

Based on US coastguard data about damage, Minorsky (**2**) has provided a useful graph which may be used for calculations based on a semi-empirical analysis; see also ref. (**4**). He bases his treatment on penetration normal to the centre-line of the struck ship and neglects components of kinetic energy parallel to it. If the mass of a stationary struck ship is m_a and that of the striking ship is m_b, then $v_b \sin \theta$ is its speed normal to the centre line of m_a where θ is the impact angle. If the two ships adhere after impact and move with speed u, see Fig. 63(a), the loss or absorption of kinetic energy is given by,

$$E_L = \tfrac{1}{2}m_b(v_b \sin \theta)^2 - \tfrac{1}{2}(m_a + m_b + m)u^2;\qquad(1)$$

m is the *added mass*† (of water) associated with the struck vessel. For the linear momentum normal to the centre-line of m_a to be conserved,

$$m_b \cdot v_b \sin \theta = (m_a + m_b + m)u.\qquad(2)$$

Eliminating u from (1) and (2), the loss of kinetic energy is

$$E_L = \frac{m_b(m_a + m)}{2(m_a + m_b + m)} \cdot (v_b \sin \theta)^2.$$

Minorsky defines a coefficient of energy absorption

$$K = \frac{m_a + m}{m_a + m_b + m}$$

so that

$$E_L = \tfrac{1}{2}m_b(v_b \sin \theta)^2 \cdot K.\qquad(3)$$

If the added mass is written as cm_a, where $0 < c < 1$,

$$K = \frac{1 + c}{1 + c + m_b/m_a} = \frac{1}{1 + M/(1 + c)} = (1 + 0{\cdot}7M)^{-1},\qquad(4)$$

where M is the mass ratio m_b/m_a with $c = 0{\cdot}4$, as assumed by Minorsky. K is not greatly altered by alterations to c of around $0{\cdot}5$.

Note that $K \to 1$ when $m_b \ll m_a$ or $M \to 0$ and when $M \to \infty$, $K \to 0$; thus if the striking ship is of relatively small mass, its energy loss is large and vice versa.

The kinetic energy loss is

$$E_L = \frac{\Delta_a \cdot \Delta_b}{1{\cdot}43\Delta_b + 2\Delta_a} \cdot (v_b \sin \theta)^2\qquad(5)$$

combining (3) and (4), and where for m_a and m_b is substituted Δ_a and Δ_b denoting the vessel displacements (usually in tons); v_b is usually in knots.

† The notion of *added mass* is treated in ref. (**5**). Briefly, the *effective* mass of a moving ship exceeds the mass of its displacement by an added mass of water which must, at the same time, also be shifted or accelerated. Observe that the upward (buoyancy) force on an ascending air bubble accelerates a certain mass of water (an added mass of volume equal to one half that of the bubble) *as well as* the (enormously smaller) mass of the bubble of air itself.

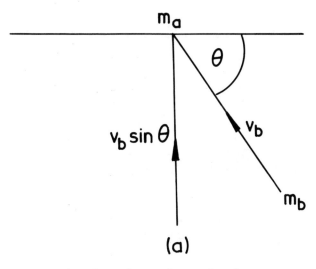

Fig. 63. (a) *Velocity diagram for two ships during impact;*

By considering in the direction of the penetration, that the decks, flats, inner and outer bottoms (but not the ship shell) are primarily energy absorbing, a resistance factor R (in units of ft² × in) is calculated, such that

$$R = \Sigma \, P_a l_a t_a + \Sigma \, P_b l_b t_b, \tag{6}$$

where P is the depth of damage (in feet) in a member, l the length (in feet) of the damage and t the thickness (in inches) (Fig. 63(b)); Σ denotes the summation of the product as it applies to plastically deformed components. Working from vessel drawings, Fig. 64 was arrived at, which is based on about 25 collisions; it gives a very useful linear correlation between R and E_L, i.e., through equation (5). Note incidentally that R *is a volume of metal undergoing significant plastic deformation*. The scatter of points at low speed collisions is due to small underestimates of speed at low impact speeds having a large effect.

A design analysis due to Jones (6-8)
Jones has made a preliminary study of how the energy of a ship collision may be dissipated by arranging for it to be absorbed either by tube or honeycomb (an example of this is seen in Fig. 65 and the note on p. 117), and he has made a comparison between them.

107

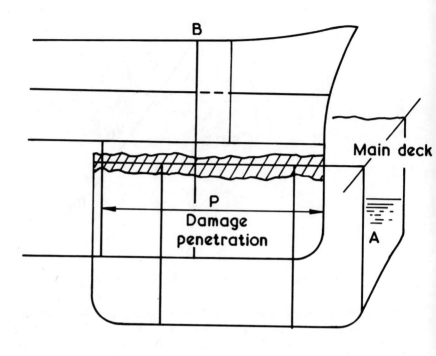

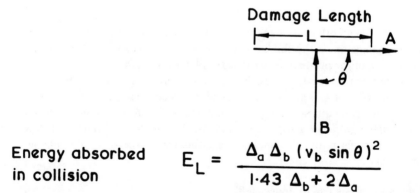

Energy absorbed in collision

$$E_L = \frac{\Delta_a \Delta_b (v_b \sin\theta)^2}{1\cdot43\,\Delta_b + 2\Delta_a}$$

(b)

Fig. 63. (b) *Damage penetration in ship collision*

108

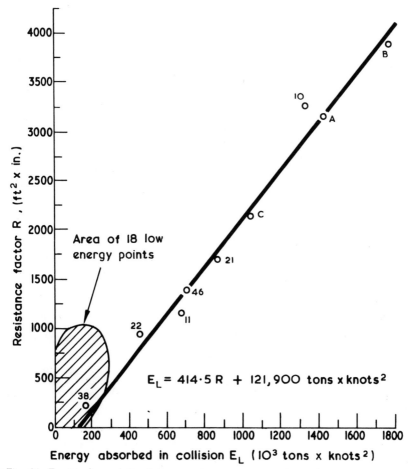

Fig. 64. *Empirical correlation between resistance to penetration and energy absorbed in collision*

An expression for the load P to cause plastic axial collapse of a thin walled tube is (13)

$$P = 6Yt_0 \sqrt{(Dt_0)}, \qquad (6)$$

where Y is the uniaxial yield stress of the material, D is the tube diameter and t_0 its thickness. For a nest of n parallel tubes for a compression distance or stroke of s, the plastic work that may be absorbed is

$$E_p = P \cdot s \cdot n$$

109

or

$$\frac{E_p}{Y \cdot V} = \frac{6t_0 \cdot ns \sqrt{(Dt_0)}}{\pi Dt_0 s \cdot n} = \frac{6}{\pi}\sqrt{\frac{t_0}{D}}, \tag{7}$$

where V is the volume of metal plastically deformed. E_p can next be equated to the kinetic energy loss as calculated following the Minorsky collision approach; i.e.,

$$\frac{E_L}{m_b v_b{}^2} = \left(2 + 1 \cdot 43 \frac{m_b}{m_a}\right)^{-1}, \tag{8}$$

and hence the number and size of tubes decided on.

The load P to cause plastic collapse for the panel of an hexagonal cell (Fig. 65), is calculated by McFarland (9) to be

$$P = 40 \cdot 5 \cdot YA \cdot (h/b)^2,$$

where h is the cell wall thickness, b the minor diameter of the cell and A the area of crushable panel, see Fig. 65. Thus the energy absorbed in crushing a panel is given by,

$$\frac{E_p}{YAs} = 40 \cdot 5 \cdot (h/b)^2, \tag{9}$$

where s is the stroke. For a honeycomb panel of $N^{\frac{1}{2}}$ cells along each side, (N is the total number of cells),

$$A = (N^{\frac{1}{2}} \cdot b)\left(2 \cdot N^{\frac{1}{2}} \cdot \frac{b}{\sqrt{3}}\right) \text{ or the volume, } V = \left(2 \cdot N \frac{b^2}{\sqrt{3}}\right)h.$$

Thus,

$$\frac{E_p}{YV} = \frac{40 \cdot 5 \cdot (h/b)^2 \cdot A \cdot s}{A \cdot h \cdot}, \text{ which with } s = b/2 \text{ gives}$$

$$\frac{E_p}{YV} = 20 \cdot 25\left(\frac{h}{b}\right). \tag{10}$$

For the same values of YV, the tube and the honeycomb can be compared thus,

$$\frac{E_p^h}{E_p^t} = \frac{20 \cdot 25h}{b}\bigg/\frac{6}{\pi}\sqrt{\frac{t}{D}} = \frac{20 \cdot 25\pi \cdot}{6}\sqrt{\frac{t}{D}} \text{ (if } h = t \text{ and } b = D)$$

$$\simeq 10\sqrt{\frac{t}{D}}. \tag{11}$$

110

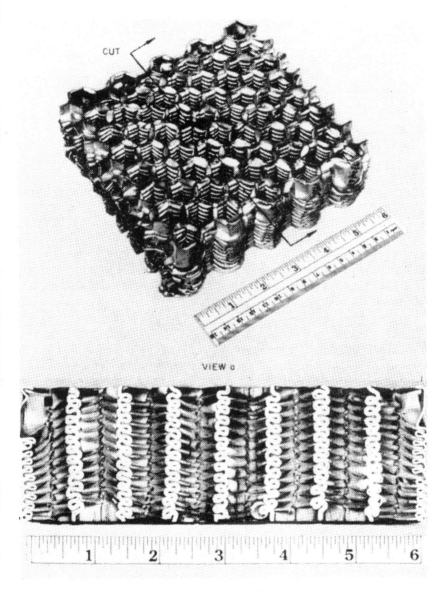

Fig. 65. Fully crushed hexagonal cell structure

111

Thus, whether tube or honeycomb is preferable depends on which side of 100 the D/t ratio lies.

From above, combining expressions for honeycomb and Minorsky's equation, i.e., $E_L = \frac{1}{2}m_b \cdot K \cdot (v_b \sin \theta)^2$

$$\text{with } \theta = 90° \text{ and } K = \frac{1}{1 + 0 \cdot 7m_b/m_a}$$

$$\text{or } \frac{E_L}{m_b v_b{}^2} = \frac{1}{2 + 1 \cdot 4m_b/m_a},$$

$$E_p = 40 \cdot 5 \cdot \left(\frac{h}{b}\right)^2 \cdot YAs = \frac{m_b v_b{}^2}{2 + 1 \cdot 4m_b/m_a}.$$

Limiting ship speed v_b is calculable when other quantities are given, as

$$v_b = \frac{40 \cdot 5(h/b) \cdot YAs(2 + 1 \cdot 4m_b/m_a)}{m_b}. \tag{12}$$

For $Y = 30\,000$ lbf/in^2, $m_a = 25\,000$ tons and $s = 1 \cdot 5$ ft (a honeycomb cell 2 ft long with a stroke-length ratio of $0 \cdot 75$) and $A = 90 \times 47 \cdot 5$ ft^2 (the value of A is similar to that for the nuclear powered ship *Otto Hahn*), equation (12) becomes

$$v_b = 476 \,(1 \cdot 4 + 2m_a/m_b)^{\frac{1}{2}} \,(h/b),$$

where v_b is in knots (1 knot $= 20 \cdot 25$ in/s), and this is plotted in Fig. 66.

Since Minorsky's work was published, a small number of other studies have appeared, and his treatment is seen now to be circumscribed in the following (6) remarks:

1. The US Naval Construction Research Establishment has evolved a useful method for predicting penetration by a *rigid bow*; only the deck plate and bottom of the struck ship are considered plastically.

2. For major collisions the analysis of Minorsky or NCRE seem appropriate, but for minor ones that due to McDermott seems preferable.

3. Akita, *et al.* (4) have observed that 'a deformation type of failure occurred when the strain directly below the bow was less than about $0 \cdot 3$, while crack-type failures are associated with larger strains'.

4. The bow structure of a striking ship is very important, and especially the strength of the side of the struck ship greatly affects the energy partition between the ships. A stiff bow (e.g., an ice-breaker) would

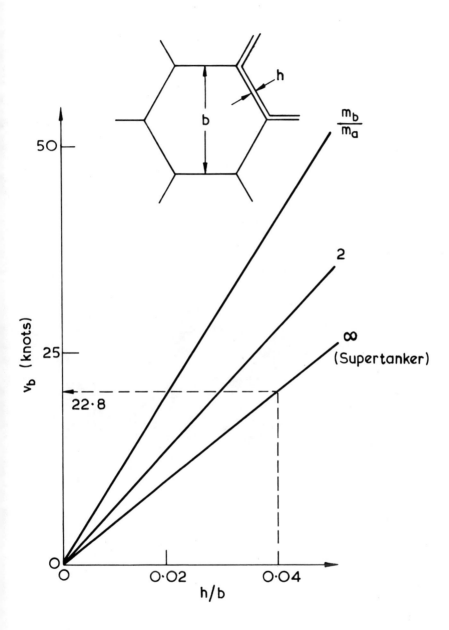

Fig. 66. Critical velocities v_b for honeycomb panels

113

absorb very little energy. Conversely, a weak bow may absorb most of the kinetic energy leaving the struck ship largely undamaged. Design requirements for nuclear-powered ships, oil-tankers, and liquid natural gas carriers are difficult to meet.

5. Minorsky's analysis, and NCRE's approach, neglect the influence of the shell plating in the struck ship and are expected to be most appropriate to major collisions. However, the shell plating behaviour of oil tankers is important for cargo containment. It is observed that 2/3 to 9/10 of the total kinetic energy in minor collisions is absorbed as membrane tension in stiffened hull plating.

Fig. 67. 'A tanker smashing into a bridge. The 11 150-ton chemical tanker Marine Floridian *crashed into a bridge at Hopewell, Virginia, hurling four cars into the James River. . . . The accident happened during the morning rush-hour as the empty tanker had a steering failure and crashed into a supporting pier of the Benjamin Harrison bridge instead of passing through the central arch. The crew tried to halt the ship's progress by dropping anchor shortly before the crash.'* (*Photo by Associated Press:* The Times, *25 February 1977*)

The stopping of moving ships (10)

Though tankers have greatly increased in size in recent years, ship service speed has remained fairly constant. However, ahead-power to displacement ratio decreases with increase in size, and since astern-power is usually a fixed proportion of ahead-power, it follows that braking power falls off with size and hence stopping-distances become proportionally greater. It is estimated that for a 165 000 ton d.w. tanker in a loaded condition initially moving at about 16 knots, a stopping distance of 2 to 4 miles and a time of 15 to 30 minutes is required. The use of brake flaps from the ship's hull, aircraft-like braking parachutes streaming in the water, and passive duct systems situated in the ship's bow have been discussed. Reversed flow from astern-running propellers often renders a vessel directionally unstable.

Figure 67 shows a small tanker crashing into a bridge; it was reported as due to a steering failure and that the crew tried in vain to prevent the crash by dropping anchor.

A more disastrous event of somewhat similar character occurred when part of the one mile long Tasman Bridge collapsed into the Derwent River after a 7200 ton freighter had collided with it (Fig. 68).

Figure 69 shows some German model testing concerning the impact behaviour of a thin hemispherical-ended, nearly conical, frustum shaped portion of bow with a rigid vertical wall, see refs (3) and (11). The plastic

Fig. 68. 'The Tasman Bridge collapse: The gap in the Tasman Bridge after a freighter had collided with it.' (Photo by Associated Press: The Guardian, *6 January 1975)*

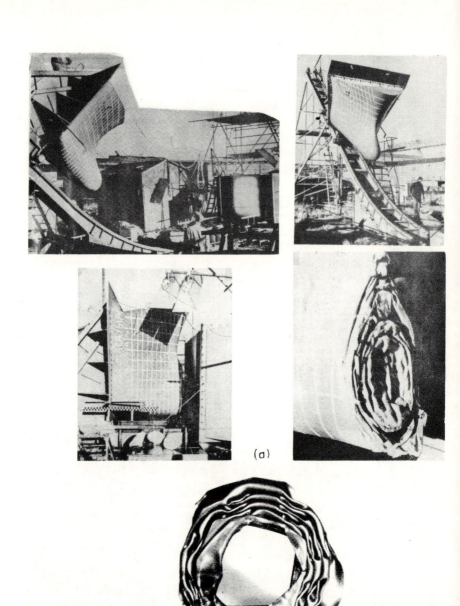

Fig. 69. (a) *Model impact testing of frustum shaped portions of a ship's bow;* (b) *Crushed shape of a conical tube due to impact*

deformation in Fig. 69(a) is seen to be very similar to that found by Postlethwaite and Mills (12) when compressing an open ended conical tube (Fig. 69(b)).

A design of a dock fender†, based essentially on plastically twisting a stationary, vertical, round solid bar due to impact during berthing, has been proposed. The bar acts as a part of a pivot and is twisted by a torque bar, at the end of which are vertical timber fenders taking any impact.

An interesting study has been made by C. T. Morley (unpublished work, 1977, Cambridge University) of the damage sustained by a supply boat of about 2500 tons displacement (length 60 m) impinging side-on amidships with a concrete column of about 15 m diameter (1 m thickness). It was shown that a plastic hinge was likely when the supply boat impact speed was about 6·5 m/s (or 3·4 m/s for a tanker of length 250 m and displacement 130 000 tons). The situation was shown to be largely one of local plastic indentation with over 95 per cent of the kinetic energy being absorbed by the ship; under impact from a supply boat (at a few metres per second) the concrete column of a typical loading platform would not collapse. Morley observed that the load-indentation properties of a ship are of great importance (typically 50 MN/m penetration for the supply boat); despite the fact that these have been discussed by Japanese workers‡, McDermott et al. and a few others, there is still need for further work. (Membrane tension in plating is important at large deflections.)

Fenders were thought to be unnecessary for preventing the gross failure of concrete shafts though they might prevent surface damage of the latter and reduce ship damage. See also ref. (14).

A note on energy absorbing honeycomb
The load-deflection curve for 'Aeroweb' hexagonal honeycomb, slowly loaded in compression parallel to the cell walls is shown in Fig. 70. Once plastic collapse has been initiated at a relatively large load, further compression continues at a fairly constant load as the cell walls buckle until about only 25 per cent of the original height remains – at which point the honeycomb bottoms and behaves as a solid block. The energy absorbed is dissipated plastically, and almost no elastic recovery occurs.

Resistance to crushing a piece of honeycomb is nearly linearly related to its density and the mechanical properties of the honeycomb foil (Fig. 71).

† The Cambridge Fender and Engineering Co. Ltd.
‡ Tanker Structural Analysis for Minor Collisions', SNAME, 382 (1974).

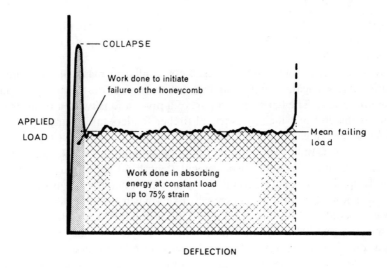

Fig. 70. Load-deflection curve for 'Aeroweb' hexagonal honeycomb statically compressed

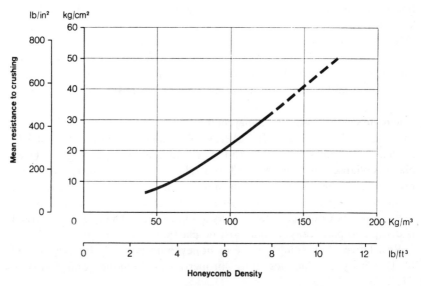

Fig. 71. Resistance to crushing versus density and mechanical properties of the honeycomb foil

118

Honeycomb in structural sandwich form is shown in Fig. 72; the skins act as do beam flanges to carry bending stress, whilst the honeycomb replaces the flange web to resist shearing load.

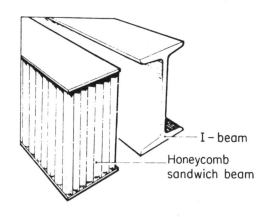

I – beam

Honeycomb
sandwich beam

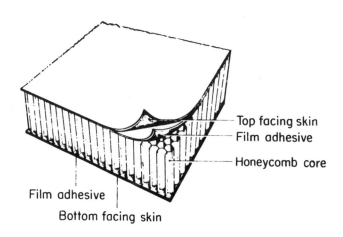

Top facing skin
Film adhesive
Honeycomb core

Film adhesive

Bottom facing skin

Fig. 72. Honeycomb in structural sandwich form

REFERENCES

(1) *Underwater Explosion Research*, Vols I, II and III 1950 (ONR London).
(2) MINORSKY, V. U., 'An Analysis of Ship·Collisions with Reference to Protection of Nuclear Power Plants', *J. of Ship Research*, 1959, **3**, 1.
(3) 'Kollisionsversuche im Schiffbau' 1974, Sonderdruck aus VDI Nachrichten, Nr. 9.
(4) AKITA, Y., and KITAMURA, K., 'A Study of Collision by an Elastic Stem to a Side Structure of a Ship', *Trans. Japan Naval Arch.* 1972, 307.
(5) BIRKHOFF, G., *Hydrodynamics* 1960 (Princeton University Press).
(6) JONES, N., 'On the Collision Protection of Ships', *Nuclear Eng. and Design* 1976, **38**, 229.
(7) JONES, N., *On the Collision Protection of Ships* 1975, Report No. 75–3, MIT, DSR. 80975.
(8) JONES, N., 'Slamming Damage', *J. of Ship Research* 1973, **17**, 80.
(9) McFARLAND, P. K., Jr, 'Hexagonal Cell Structures under Post-Buckling Axial Load', *AIAA Journal* 1963, **1**, 1380.
(10) CLARKE, D., and WELLMAN, F., *The Stopping of Large Tankers and the Feasibility of Using Auxiliary Braking Devices* 1970 (Roy. Inst. Naval Architects).
(11) JOHNSON, W., and MAMALIS, A. G., 'Gegenüberstellung statischer und dynamischer Schadens- oder Deformationserscheinungen', *Fortschritt-Berichte der VDI-Z*, 1977, Reihe 5, No. 32.
(12) POSTLETHWAITE, H. E., and MILLS, B., 'Use of Collapsible Structural Elements as Impact Isolators, with Special Reference to Automotive Applications', *J. Strain Analysis*, 1970, **5**, 58.
(13) ALEXANDER, J. M., 'An Approximate Analysis of the Collapse of Thin Cylindrical Shells under Axial Loading', *Q.J. Mech. Appl. Math.*, 1960, **13**, 10.

Part V: Lift or elevator crashes

The Accident at Markham Colliery, Derbyshire, UK (1)

On 30 July 1973, 18 men were killed, and 11 seriously injured, when a cage carrying them crashed into the coalpit bottom as a result of an over-wind; at impact it fractured 17 wooden landing baulks. The shaft down which the cage fell was 4·6 m (15 ft) diameter, was brick-lined and the pit bottom at 429 m (1407 ft). Double-deck cages, for a maximum of 16 persons on each, were in operation. Both the ropes and the capel were pulled over the headgear pulley and fell down on top of, and alongside, the cage containing the men. The disaster was due to the complete failure of the winding engine brake; the centre rod of the spring nest fractured, believed to be due to fatigue. The bottom deck of the cage was severely distorted but there was little damage to the top deck (Fig. 73); the speed of impact was estimated at 43·4 km/h (27 miles/h).

In the conclusions of the official report on this disaster, it is stated, 'the fatal or serious injuries received by the men in the descending cage were caused by it crashing on to the wooden baulks at the bottom of the shaft. The accident would not have been so serious if, instead of landing baulks, an arresting device had been installed below the lowest winding level.' A recommendation followed to the effect that 'all *solid landings* in shafts be replaced by suitable arresting devices below the lowest winding level as soon as possible'.

Arresting devices

Many kinds of energy absorbing devices would be suitable as pit-cage arresters. One such device (2) (for some design calculations see Appendix 1) consists of a frame carrying four (mean yield stress $\sim$ 324 N/mm² (21 tonf/in²)) strips of mild steel, about 6·4 × 1650 mm (0·25 in × 65 in), the strips being bent and unbent around a total of twenty rolls, 76 mm (3 in) diameter. In pulling the strip between the rolls, any kinetic energy is dissipated in plastically bending and unbending the strip. The rolls are carried on a movable saddle which can be pushed up and down a frame; each of the four strips would be attached to a corner of the frame. The load absorbed, per roll in the full scale device, is about 16 kN (1·6 tons). A system of these proportions was arrived at for bringing to rest a cage of weight 230 kN (23 tons) initially moving at 9 m/s (30 ft/s) in 3·65 m (12 ft), i.e., at a rate of 1·13 g.

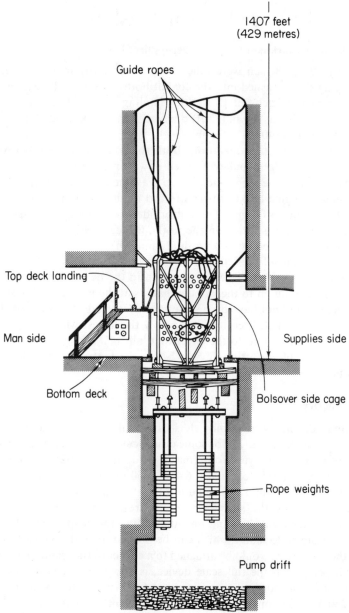

1407 feet
(429 metres)

Guide ropes

Top deck landing

Man side

Supplies side

Bottom deck

Bolsover side cage

Rope weights

Pump drift

Fig. 73. Section of the pit bottom

122

A simple system in which a falling cage would impinge on, and thus crush, several layers of thin wall tube – alternate layers of parallel tubes being orthogonal – is indicated in ref. (3) along with a useful design curve derived from experimental investigations. For a discussion of potentially useful energy absorbing devices see refs (4), (5) and (6).

REFERENCES

(1) Cmd 5557, 1974, HMSO. Report presented to British Parliament.
(2) Private communication from Professor ALEXANDER, J. M., refers to the 'Selda' linear energy absorber (13 June 1977), then in the design stage.
(3) JOHNSON, W., REID, S. R., and REDDY, T. Y., 'The Compression of Crossed Layers of Thin Tubes', *Int. J. Mech. Sci.*, 1977, **19**, 423.
(4) JOHNSON, W., *Impact Strength of Materials* 1972 (Arnold, London).
(5) EZRA, A. A., and FAY, R. J., *Dynamic Response of Structures* 1972, p. 205. Eds HERRMANN, G., and PERRONE, N. (Pergamon Press, Oxford).
(6) JOHNSON, W., and REID, S. R., 'Metallic Energy Dissipating Systems' 1978. Review to be published in *Applied Mechanics Reviews*.

APPENDIX 1

Approximate theory for plastic bending and unbending over a roll

For a fairly wide rectangular strip of width w and thickness t of radius R (where $t/R \ll 1$) and such that there is no friction between the roll and the strip (Fig. 74), then the excess of tension $\Delta T = T_o - T_i$, where T_o is the tension on the outgoing side and T_i that on the ingoing side (assuming that T, T_o, $T_i \ll 2wt\,Y$), is related through a plastic work equation by,

$$2M_P \frac{v}{R + t/2} = \Delta(T_o - T_i)v; \text{ or } \Delta(T_o - T_i) = \frac{wt^2 \cdot Y}{2R + t}. \tag{1}$$

M_P is the full plastic bending moment (with tension) $\simeq wt^2 Y/4$, where Y is the mean yield stress† and v/R is the rate of bending of the strip; the two on the left of the equation occurs because the process is one of bending *and* unbending.

The effect of the tension on the strip, as it passes over a roll, is to elongate it. The mean residual tensile strain acquired by the strip in passing over a roll is

$$e_R \simeq 4 \cdot \Delta a/(2R + t). \tag{2}$$

Distance Δa refers to the plastic stress 'blocks' over the strip section when mean tension $T = (T_o + T_i)/2$ is present and its meaning will be evident from Fig. 74(b). We then have,

$$(T_o + T_i)/2 = T = 2w \cdot \Delta a \cdot Y \text{ or } \Delta a = T/2w\,Y. \tag{3}$$

Assume a proposed test rig has a strip thickness of 6·4 mm (0·25 in), width 152 mm (6 in) and passes over a rod of 76 mm (3 in) diameter, and that the mean yield stress may be assumed to be 340 N/mm² (22 tonf/in²). Then, if $T_i = 0$, we have $T_o = wt^2 Y/(2R + t) = 6 \times (1/16) \times 22/3 \cdot 25 = 25 \cdot 3$ kN (2·54 tonf) or $T = T_o/2 = 2 \cdot 54/2 = 12 \cdot 7$ kN (1·27 tonf). $\Delta a = T_o/4w\,Y = 1 \cdot 27/(2 \times 6 \times 22) = 0 \cdot 13$ mm (0·0052 in) and $e_R = 4\Delta a/(2R + t) = 4 \times 0 \cdot 0052/3 \cdot 25 = 0 \cdot 0064$.

---

† The bending and unbending is essentially under plane strain conditions if $w \gg t$. For a strip material whose uniaxial stress/strain curve is $\sigma = A(B + \epsilon)^n$

$$\bar{\sigma} \simeq \int_0^{\epsilon_m} A(B + \epsilon)^n d\epsilon/\epsilon_m,$$

if the extreme fibre stress is ϵ_m; and then $Y = 2\sqrt{(3)}\,\bar{\sigma}/3$

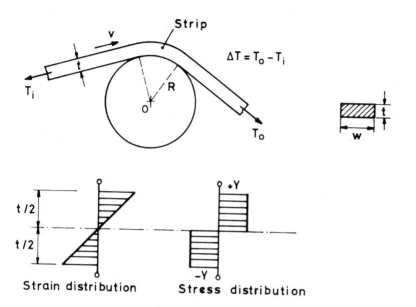

(a) Pure bending : no tension

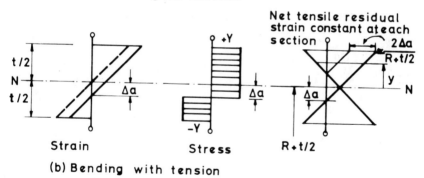

(b) Bending with tension

Fig. 74. *Plastic bending and unbending over a roll*

AUTHOR INDEX

Note: Page numbers in bold type indicate reference at the ends of parts.

126

127

SUBJECT INDEX